# THE CLASSICAL REVOLT

# The Classical Revolt

RACHEL TERRY

# Contents

Edited by Eva Terry.
Cover art by Rachel and Eva Terry with assistance from Midjourney.
First Printing, 2024

For Ben, Rebecca, Spencer, Eva,
Jace, Kerrigan, Alex, Tommy, and Piper

# Introduction

*August 2014, Lincoln, Nebraska—*

Our household buzzed with the nerves and excitement of a new school year. There were errands to run (clarinet reeds, swim goggles, athletic physicals) and lunches to pack. Permission slips and textbooks piled up on the kitchen table. We were an utterly normal family doing perfectly normal things. And then that fateful email arrived.

The teachers at Irving Middle School had received handouts at their kick-off training that advised them against calling children "boys" and "girls." Instead, they could use alternatives like "campers" or "purple penguins." Several teachers quietly objected but felt they couldn't stage any resistance without risking their jobs. One teacher emailed the handouts to me and asked if I could rally some parents to address the issue at a school board meeting.

It felt impossible. I'd never been to a school board meeting before and didn't know many people. We'd only lived in Lincoln for two years. Still, I managed to scrape together 70 email addresses of friends, neighbors, and acquaintances, hoping to amass a group of concerned parents.

I wrote a 5-minute speech and attached it to the email along with copies of the infamous handouts. Nervously, I pressed send, unsure of what would follow.

The phone rang, and instead of what I expected (a friend asking questions about the school board meeting), it was the education reporter for the *Lincoln Journal Star*. She had somehow obtained my email (she wouldn't tell me how) and wanted to discuss my intentions.

"I'd rather just talk to the school board," I told her. "It doesn't seem fair to me that they should hear this through the newspaper first."

"Whether or not you talk to me, we're going to do a story," she said. And sure enough, I found myself in the newspaper the next day. Since I hadn't answered the reporter's questions, she printed excerpts from the sample speech I'd included in my email to other parents.

Major news outlets picked up the story, and soon, I was fielding phone calls from *National Review* and *Fox News*. I did a live interview on *Fox & Friends*. The limo, the studio, the host's voice in my earpiece—these were all surreal experiences for a small-town mom.

The day of the school board meeting finally arrived, and the school district office was a circus. News crews lined the walls, and so many people crammed into the main room that they opened an overflow in the basement. Someone offered me his seat so I could be up toward the front, and I sat down. People pointed at me, and several walked up to me and introduced themselves. Let me remind you that I was not a public figure. I was a mom who was concerned about something going on at her daughter's school.

I had been a mother for seventeen years at this point. I'd learned to protect my children in many small ways: shielding their eyes from violence on a screen or teaching them how to face bullies on the playground. But this was when I realized that much of school education had morphed into indoctrination. I'd thought school was a place for my children to fine-tune their reading comprehension and conquer geometry. Suddenly, school felt like a battleground.

The public schools had become Ground Zero in the growing culture wars. It made sense: the hearts and minds of the rising generation are up for grabs.

## How and why I wrote this book

The once-foreign concepts of 2014 have entered the mainstream. Today, the gender spectrum shocks no one. We're saturated with it. Over the past decade, inherited societal norms have been recklessly discarded and trampled upon. Academic theories have exacerbated racial tensions in the United States and infiltrated classrooms from coast to coast. Unexpectedly, schools have been forced to shut their doors—a reality I had never anticipated nor considered. Equally shockingly, public health experts have encouraged parents to expose their children to untested drug therapies. Furthermore, TikTok has become a vehicle for dangerous messaging directly into our children's hands.

Amid these challenges, the 2020 school closures provided parents a revealing glimpse into what's happening (and not happening) in classrooms. Armed with this newfound awareness, parents are on alert. But the question remains: How do we ensure quality education for our children in a world that is more focused on sexuality and politics than reading and math?

My motivation for writing this book stems from a decade of active involvement in these discussions. I've authored articles and blog posts, appeared on radio and television, engaged with superintendents and legislators, pursued a school board position, and founded a school choice organization.

However, my most impactful work took place within the walls of my own home. Early on, I realized that delegating my children's educations had unforeseen consequences. With a limited budget that excluded private schooling, we ventured into various educational avenues: charter schools, homeschooling, college courses, homeschool co-ops, online classes, and more.

Today, one of our children is enrolled in college; the other two have successfully graduated and are embarking on building their own families. I no longer receive emails from teachers about questionable teacher training sessions. Instead, I'm contemplating the educational future of my grandchildren.

As a testament to my commitment, I have also returned to college to pursue a Master's in Rhetoric and Composition. The embryonic critical theories I encountered during my undergraduate years in the 1990s have since burgeoned into queer theory and performativity. Online pundits may relegate critical theory to a law school subject, but its influence extends far beyond that limited realm. Critical theory's pervasive impact has spread to every facet of our culture and has derailed K-12 education.

I hope that by the time you reach the final page of this short book, you will feel a sense of clarity about the path forward for your children's education. And I also hope you'll have the confidence to follow your instincts.

## How this book will benefit you

I began writing solely from my own perspective but quickly recognized the need for a broader outlook. So I've interviewed parents, educators, and researchers in the United States and other Western nations. Through their stories, you'll discover that you're not alone in your concerns about K-12 "education."

Further, you'll see that your concerns naturally fall into three distinct categories: protection, preparation, and paideia. Even if the term "paideia" is unfamiliar, its essence has likely been a concern of yours all along. I only recently encountered this term as I immersed myself in classical education—the system our ancestors honed and perfected over centuries, if not millennia. This type of education yielded the awe-inspiring cathedrals of Europe, the dissemination of literature via printing presses, and the crafting of the Declaration of Independence. Today, the demand for this style of education is arguably more pressing than ever before. As Michelle Kelso Kafer, a homeschooling mother in Tennessee, said during our conversation, "Yes, technology has evolved, but the core of humanity remains unchanged."

At the conclusion of each chapter, you'll encounter a summary of the covered topics and a segment called "Go Deeper." This book is tailored to be a swift and accessible read because parents are busy. However, if you want to explore specific subjects in more detail, the references provided in the "Go Deeper" sections stand ready to guide you.

Ultimately, I hope this book will leave you with this: your deliberate focus on your children's education will yield a lasting impact on the world. One child capable of discerning truth becomes a beacon on a hill. And in these challenging times, we need more light!

## A hydra-of-a-problem

One person you'll meet in this book is Gabrielle Clark. As we discussed K-12 in our interview, she said, "This is a hydra of a problem." Let's briefly revisit the story of the Hydra.

In ancient Greek mythology, Hercules confronted the Hydra, a serpent-like creature with multiple heads. Hercules and his nephew Iolaus tried to defeat the creature, but they realized that decapitating the Hydra merely caused fresh heads to sprout.

Hercules sliced through the heads with his sword while Iolaus burned the wounds to thwart regrowth. In the climax, they defeated all heads but one—the immortal head. Overcoming this final hurdle, Hercules buried the immortal head beneath an immense boulder, rendering it impotent. You may not see yourself as Hercules, but you are a hero to your children in many ways. When you finish this book, you'll be teeming with strategies to staunch the wounds and maybe even incapacitate the ultimate hydra head beneath a weighty stone, rendering it powerless against your children's well-being.

From bullying and data collection to Marxism and grade inflation, the hydra of mis-education in America has many heads. As Gabrielle Clark said, you can't focus on just one problem and hope everything will turn out okay.

The tools necessary to guide your children through their formative years, equipping them for a life enriched with self-sufficiency, contentment, faith, and curiosity, reside within you. Let's get started!

## Chapter 1

# Families are the building blocks of society

In April 24, 2010, the phone rang in Nikki Bradshaw Carpenter's Jackson, Mississippi, mobile home. The caller told her a storm was headed her way. Nikki gathered her three young sons (seven-year-old Layne, two-year-old Ethan, and one-year-old Austin) and led them to the trailer's hallway. She piled all the household's pillows on top of them and then threw her 115-pound frame over the pile.

The storm arrived with ferocity, unleashing 170-mph winds that uprooted Carpenter's trailer, flinging it over a hundred yards. Neighbors heard the boys crying and searched through the wreckage. Tragically, Nikki's sacrifice came at a heart-wrenching cost—the tornado broke her back and neck. Layne suffered a fractured hand, and Ethan's right ear required surgery, but baby Austin was miraculously unhurt. Layne later told his grandfather that he "heard his little brothers calling out for her, and when she didn't answer, he knew she was gone because she always answered when they called."

What drives a mother to sacrifice her life to protect her children? Why is the family the cornerstone of human society? And who would seek to sever the unbreakable bond between children and their protectors?

Most of us will never find ourselves in a situation like Nikki's. Few parents have to throw themselves over their children to protect them from a tornado's fury. But a storm has been brewing in our culture for some time now. And the stakes are growing higher and higher. Are you willing to do what it takes to keep your children safe?

## Families are the building blocks of society

Before we go on, I want to zoom out and broaden our perspective a bit. The position of the family within societies has not always been stable. Right now, it feels shaky because of relentless attacks, but it hasn't always been that way.

In 1989, the United Nations recognized the family as the foundational unit of a civilized society, marking 1994 as the inaugural "International Year of the Family." Its motto succinctly encapsulated this sentiment: "Building the smallest democracy at the heart of society."

The late 80s and early 90s were marked by sweeping global changes. Authoritarian regimes were collapsing at an unprecedented rate. The Philippines overthrew its communist dictator in 1986. In 1988, the Estonian Soviet Socialist Republic declared sovereignty. And, in the aftermath of the Chernobyl disaster, multiple Soviet states saw opportunities to sever ties.

In South Korea, by June 1987, student demonstrators successfully toppled a military dictatorship. Come August 1989, Poland elected Tadeusz Mazoweicki, an anti-communist Catholic editor, as their Prime Minister. With no protest from the Soviet Union, by 1990, the Republic of Poland was established with Lech Walesa as its president. Inspired by Poland, Hungary began to dismantle its border fence with Austria in

1989. By the 33rd anniversary of the 1956 Revolution, Hungary had abolished its communist regime.

November saw the Berlin Wall crumble, symbolizing the reunification of Germany in October 1990. The Velvet Revolution in Czechoslovakia emerged as a peaceful transition, culminating in Vaclav Havel, a once-imprisoned playwright for anti-communist sentiments, becoming president in December 1989.

However, not all movements for freedom were without casualty. Protests in China's Tiananmen Square led to military crackdown, and while the Communist party persisted, the event catalyzed significant economic reforms in the country.

Between 1989 and 1991, previously communist nations across Europe and Asia held democratic elections. The culmination came with the dissolution of the Soviet Union by the end of 1991, marking a significant ideological shift.

The wave of transformation wasn't confined to these regions. Countries in Africa, Asia, and South America, including Mali, Burkina Faso, South Yemen, and Nicaragua, to name just a few, dismissed and abandoned Marxist ideologies during the late 1980s and early 1990s.

The surge in democratic principles and the UN's recognition of the family's significance aren't mere coincidence. In times of upheaval—whether political, economic, or natural—society often retreats to its most fundamental unit: the family.

## Why are families so critical?

When governments fail and economies collapse, families pick up the pieces. We see this every time there's an emergency. When schools shut down in March 2020, where did the students go? They went home. Even though schools had been conditioning parents to rely on them to serve breakfast and lunch and care for the children after school, the moment an emergency arose, it was up to parents to figure things out. Why are families so critical to the survival of the human race?

### *Socialization*

Before birth, babies recognize their parents' voices, establishing a connection to the outside world. Families impart cultural values, beliefs, and customs. Children gain a sense of identity from their place in the family. And the day-in-day-out interactions form the basis of interpersonal skills and conflict resolution.

### *Emotional Support*

The world presents challenges even to the young. In the face of adversity, like schoolyard bullies, a supportive family acts as an emotional anchor, helping children navigate these tumultuous waters.

### *Economic Support*

Beyond emotional sustenance, families often provide material support, pooling resources for mutual benefit. They also form invaluable social networks that can guide children in their professional pursuits.

### *Social Stability*

Families foster social stability by instilling virtues like discipline, integrity, and responsibility. These teachings, passed from parent to child, reinforce societal strength.

In essence, families are society's bedrock. Prioritizing their stability and the relationships within is paramount. However, concerning trends are emerging that seek to strain these bonds. The question then becomes: what drives these divisive agendas?

## Marxism and strong families are incompatible

Way back in the 1800s, socialists like Karl Marx and August Bebel in Germany and Charles Fcurier and Robert Owen in Great Britain thought the traditional family posed several significant problems to their Marxist ideology:

1. Families provide financial security. It's difficult to eliminate private property when children can receive inheritances from their parents, uncles, aunts, or grandparents and when family members can pool their resources and help one another.
2. It's challenging to indoctrinate children when their parents teach them.
3. A traditional home life is typically incompatible with sexual promiscuity.

Marx and Engels wanted to replace home education with social education, which meant learning from the community instead of solely the family. They didn't just mean sending kids to public school but also having national institutions where children could be cared for and educated at the country's expense. Engels even said that children should be raised together in these institutions as soon as they were weaned.

Today, Marxist regimes advocate for the government to take a more significant role in raising children instead of their parents for several reasons. One of the main reasons is to ensure that children are presented with a consistent ideological outlook that aligns with Marxist beliefs. If the state can oversee the education and socialization of children, they can mold the younger generation into loyal adherents of their ideology and ensure that the next generation carries on their ideas. The LGBTQ agenda is a perfect way to break down the family. In fact, with transgender surgeries, ideologues ensure that people don't even have a chance to bear and raise their own children in the future.

Marxist thought views families as private institutions reinforcing individualistic values and distracting individuals from their collective duties to the state. By having the government take on the child-rearing role, ideologues can diminish the importance of the traditional family structure and promote a more communal approach to child-rearing. In such a scenario, children are raised to serve the state, not their families.

Lastly, Marxist regimes view the family as a potential obstacle to their authority. By separating children from their parents and encouraging them to identify more with the state than their families, they can reduce the likelihood of dissent and resistance to their rule.

But it can't be easy to separate children from their parents. Can it? Americans have paid for government schools with their property and income taxes for generations. Our money goes directly to the local district schools, whether we choose to send our children there or not. And increasingly, we see that public schools indoctrinate children in Marxist ideology, often at the expense of academic subjects.

Additionally, political organizations have successfully gotten parents to take their children to indoctrination events dressed up as something else. Drag Queen Story Hour has been one of the most controversial parenting topics of the last few years, and for good reason. In 2020, Harris Kornstein and Harper Keenan published an academic article in *Curriculum In-*

*quiry* called "Drag Pedagogy: The playful practice of queer imagination in early childhood."[1] This article has been used by many organizations to justify the funding and development of organizations that introduce children to Marxist queer theory.

Kornstein is a humanities professor at the University of Arizona, and he also likes to perform as a drag queen called "Lil Miss Hot Mess." Keenan is a professor of gender and sexuality research in education at the University of British Columbia. They're not shy about what the non-profit Drag Queen Story Hour (DQSH) hopes to accomplish.

Their journal article explains, "It may be that DQSH is 'family friendly,' in the sense that it is accessible and inviting to families with children, but it is less a sanitizing force than it is a preparatory introduction to alternate modes of kinship. Here, DQSH is 'family friendly' in the sense of 'family' as an old-school queer code to identify and connect with other queers on the street." In other words, they're grooming children to be queer and preparing them for the deconstruction of the traditional family ("alternate modes of kinship").

Why you would take your child to learn from people who want to destroy your family is beyond me. But it's happening, and we parents must do everything we can to protect our children from those who wish to use them to gain power. It's time to throw ourselves on top of the pillows piled on our children. The storm is already raging.

## Summary

- Parents care about their children more than anyone else.
- Families are the building blocks of society.
- Marxist ideology is incompatible with strong, traditional families.
- There are forces at work in today's society that are trying to break the bonds between parents and children.

### Go Deeper

In the autumn of 2020, Christopher F. Rufo published a deep dive into Drag Queen Story Hour (DQSH). Already a cultural flashpoint, the drag events for children seemed to have come out of nowhere. But Rufo connects the dots in this article: "The Real Story Behind Drag Queen Story Hour." It's well worth the read: https://www.city-journal.org/article/the-real-story-behind-drag-queen-story-hour

# Chapter 2

# Trust the Experts

This is a book about education, but we need to back up. Long before you register your child for preschool or kindergarten, you're conditioned to doubt yourself and "trust the experts."

Case in point:

During my first pregnancy, I felt that something was wrong. My legs were very swollen, and eventually, so were my hands and face. Friends didn't even recognize me when they saw me on the street. When I told my doctor that I thought I might have pre-eclampsia, he brushed me off. "You're just swollen because it's summer," he said.

He was wrong. A nurse caught the problem during a false labor hospital visit. What followed was a harrowing whirlwind, leading to complications and a difficult first month for our newborn daughter.

Let's face it. Women are notoriously easy to scare into submission where their children are concerned, and, unfortunately, practitioners and providers in many industries have figured this out.

## Birth practices

Parenting begins before birth. As soon as you see that pink line on the pregnancy test, your life is never the same. You're already caring for that child through every bite, every nap, every breath. A woman's pregnancy experiences influence her readiness to face the challenges of motherhood, and when she's treated as if she doesn't know anything, she develops the habit of relying on "experts" instead of her own judgment.

Studies show that when women give birth without unnecessary inventions, they experience a "transformative psychological experience that generates a sense of empowerment."[2] When you're faced with the responsibility of caring for a brand-new helpless human, you need to feel powerful. But in the United States, more than 3 in 10 births is a Caesarean section, and more than 7 in 10 includes an epidural.[3]

Why would so many women opt for invasive interventions that result in their feeling less powerful as parents? The following rhetoric, from WebMD, helps us understand why: "Childbirth is one of the most painful experiences many people go through in life. Pushing a baby out of your birth canal pushes your body to its physical limits. Labor and delivery can last hours or days and involve painful contractions, stretching, tear, and pressure." Boy, that sounds bad! Isn't there anything to solve this terrible problem?

After explaining the pros and cons (mostly pros) of the procedure, the WebMD article concludes, "Epidurals during childbirth are a common, effective, and overall safe procedure that gives you quick pain relief or temporary numbness. It's natural to feel anxious about the delivery process. You shouldn't be afraid to ask your OBGYN any questions you might have about childbirth."

The article does mention "rare risks" that can come from the procedure, which include permanent neurological damage, chronic pain, and permanent paralysis. But it doesn't mention that you'll miss out on the exhilarating experience of withstanding pain for your child and being an active participant in the amazing work your body will do as you bring a baby into the world.

Also, when you subject yourself to an epidural, you're stuck in bed for a while after the birth. If there's anything wrong with the baby, you must watch the nurses whisk the child away, and you can't follow because your legs are useless until the drug wears off.

Sometimes complications are unavoidable, and you just get through the delivery any way you can. But our current US system puts way too many births in this category.

As I mentioned earlier, nearly 32% of US babies are delivered cesarean. How does that compare to other countries? Finland, Iceland, and Norway have C-section rates around 15%, due to high quality midwifery care, different legal attitudes toward medical litigation, and strict guidelines about elective cesarean deliveries.[4]

The American system, with its high rate of medical interventions during childbirth, exemplifies a broader trend where parents are conditioned to entrust their child's welfare almost exclusively to professionals, often at the expense of their own natural abilities and instincts. It is a poignant reminder that how we begin the journey of parenthood has profound, lasting effects on our confidence and approach as caregivers, and it underscores the need for a cultural shift towards empowering parents, right from the start.

From the beginning of your pregnancy, realize that birth is instinctive and doesn't need to be taught. Your body is prepared to nurture and deliver a baby. It has magnificent muscles, powerful cells, and even the milk-producing glands necessary for feeding your child after birth.

Some practitioners treat pregnant women like patients who are ill; others simply tell you what to expect in the coming month and run tests on you. You need someone who will listen to your concerns, answer your questions, and reassure you that you have what it takes to successfully carry and deliver your baby.

According to Dr. Robert S. Mendelsohn, doctors in Europe had a difficult time co-opting childbirth during the 18th century. They knew if they could, they'd have a steady stream of income. But it wasn't an easy sell. After all, women had been delivering children without doctors' help since the beginning of time. He explained, "In order to get their hands on all those patients, the doctors *had* to convert childbirth into a disease. They did it by interfering with the natural process and creating medical interventions that only they could perform."[5]

Keep this concept in mind: some "experts" find that if they convert a natural part of life into a disease (or a problem), they can get people to pay them to fix it. This happens in education all the time.

## Conflicts of interest

American culture is infatuated with innovation and progress, and we've benefitted enormously from this fascination. No other country in the world enjoys a higher standard of living, and commonplace medical treatments here are only available to the wealthy in other nations.

I appreciate these innovations, but I also recognize that we put ourselves and our children at risk when we're all-in with the latest medical innovations before they've been tried and tested over time. Throughout most of history, young mothers turned to their own mothers and grandmothers for advice when raising children. Today, even if our mothers and grandmothers live down the street, we usually turn to "experts." I'm not saying there's anything wrong with this, necessarily, but it's important to keep conflicts of interest in the back of your mind when you're seeking advice.

Family members, friends, and neighbors don't have a conflict of interest when it comes to your child and advice. They have a lot invested in your child, and they want what's best for your family.

But many of the people we deem "experts" do have conflicts of interest.

Although pharmaceutical kickbacks are illegal, FDA and court documents show that they do indeed happen. Some doctors, such as Florida Doctor Anthony Baldizzi,[6], prescribe certain drugs in exchange for luxury vehicles supplied by pharmaceutical marketers. And companies like Pacira Pharmaceuticals, Inc.,[7] have paid kickbacks to doctors in the form of bogus research grants.

With the opaque state of medical billing, it's unlikely that these kinds of schemes will disappear anytime soon, but you don't have to let your children be the unnecessary victims of these "experts." If you're unsure about a particular prescription, do some research yourself or get a second opinion. And remember that there's a lot of money and influence up for grabs for "experts" who solve problems.

But conflicts of interest are relegated to the medical domain, right? How could that happen in K-12 education?

When I ran for school board in Lincoln, Nebraska, the superintendent requested a meeting with me—standard procedure, his secretary said. During our conversation, he confessed that the district was facing a difficult problem. Kawasaki had donated a significant sum for a new building because the superintendent had promised a steady stream of young people trained in welding. But now, students weren't signing up. The superintendent racked his brain, trying to figure out how to get students to uphold his end of the bargain with Kawasaki. He had a conflict of interest. When people have such conflicts, they cease to see people as individuals with lives of their own. Instead, they see them as pawns in their own schemes.

## Kindergarten round-up

"Kindergarten round-up" perfectly describes the government school system's view of children—more like cattle than individual human beings. All the five-year-olds in the neighborhood get rounded up and assigned to a classroom in the local school, whether they're ready to be away from home or not. In the last couple of decades, full-day kindergarten has largely replaced half-day, even though child development hasn't changed. The conveyor belt system of education in the United States shuffles children along in age groups regardless of their skills, talents, and interests.

You know your five-year-old better than anyone else does. You certainly know him better than the principal at the local school. Also, you probably have ideas about what kind of learning environment would best suit your child.

If you grew up attending a district public school, you know the environment. It's common to find checklists online to help you know if your child is "ready for school." Most criteria centers on whether your child is ready to comply with the government school environment. You'll see items like these on such lists:

- Can your child listen to instructions and follow them?
- Can he go to the bathroom by himself?
- Can he cut with scissors?
- Does he know how to take turns?
- Can he hold a pencil?

But starting full-day government school at age five may not be the best situation for your child. Children who are not developmentally ready to read at age five might develop a dislike for school that can be difficult to overcome. In Finland, which has one of the most successful education systems in the world, children don't begin school until age 7.

The current system of kindergarten enrollment, where children are grouped solely based on age, disregards their individual readiness, skills, talents, and interests, treating them more like commodities than unique individuals. As a parent, you have a deep understanding of your own child and have the right to choose an environment that would truly suit their needs, rather than send them off to a one-size-fits-all approach imposed by the government school system.

## Public health

Pediatric health care has evolved significantly in recent generations. One notable outcome of this evolution is a growing perception that parents are increasingly treated as if they are uninformed. During "well-child visits," pediatricians do more than just examine patients; they also dispense extensive advice. This marks a departure from the traditional role of doctors as professionals who are consulted as needed, transforming them into figures who dictate when appointments are required and how parents should raise their children.

Consider other professions, such as plumbers or accountants. People hire them for specific tasks, like fixing a pipe or preparing tax returns. Imagine the frustration if a plumber insisted on regular, paid pipe inspections, or if an accountant began directing personal spending habits.

Pediatrics became a distinct medical specialty in the early 1900s. By the mid-1800s, many of the primary causes of child mortality, such as contagious diseases and malnutrition, had been largely addressed. Thereafter, pediatricians increasingly focused on the care of healthy children. In 1983, the American Academy of Pediatrics sought to increase child check-up visits by 50%, from 14 to 21 visits—a decision that was, and still is, debated among healthcare professionals.[8]

Some critics liken well-child visits to subscription services, akin to Amazon Prime. These scheduled visits provide doctors with consistent income, yet the health benefits for children are not always clear. A 2008 study found that well-child visits can inadvertently expose healthy children to illnesses present in the clinic, effectively facilitating the spread of disease. For example, nearly 800,000 children in 2008 contracted influenza-like illnesses during well-child visits, imposing a hefty cost of $500 million annually.[9]

One increasingly common policy—such as that recently adopted by Honor Health in Arizona—is granting adolescents the ability to manage their own medical information and potentially revoke parental access.[10][11] This policy disregards the wealth of knowledge parents have about their child's medical history, from past allergic reactions to childhood injuries, and positions them on the sidelines of their child's healthcare. This approach is not only counter-intuitive but potentially hazardous.

Today's parents are often navigating a landscape where they may feel pressured by the advice of healthcare professionals, leading to a dynamic where they might feel obliged to follow doctors' orders unquestioningly. After all, doctors are the experts, and new parents are typically seen as child-rearing rookies. However, no matter their credentials, no one knows a child as intimately as their parents, and no one loves them as dearly.

## Early childhood case study

Another way to make money off new, unsure parents is to create programs that send "experts" into their homes. While there may be some cases in which parents need to learn basic child-care skills, programs like these can be worse than invasive. They can convey the idea that parents don't have what it takes to be good moms and dads. Further, they can communicate the message that to be a good parent, you must do what the state tells you to do.

Let's practice looking at messaging from organizations that would like more power over families. The following X campaign was launched by Nebraska Loves Public Schools in 2016.

In this tweet, NElovesPS reminds parents that "little ones don't come with a set of instructions when they're born." How often have parents lamented this fact.

When parents repeat this common phrase, they often talk about how different their children are. You finally figure out how to motivate your oldest child to eat broccoli and then you realize that the same methods don t work at all with her younger brother. But that doesn't seem to be what NElovesPS is talking about here. They suggest that if you're unclear about how to be a good parent (starting "the moment a child is born"), you should ask Crete Public Schools for help.

There are undoubtedly some very wise and good people working for Crete Public Schools. But the suggestion that they know what's best for every child and that they know better than their parents is just silly (and insulting to the parents).

Here's another: "The most promising approach to #earlyed is one that involves parents directly." And don't forget: "Most parents want to be great parents." They *want* to, but they just don't have what it takes.

The ad's photo shows two parents, a baby, and a woman showing them a picture on an iPad. It appears that the woman with the iPad is a visitor to the home, but she's presented as the expert. Her body language, her position to the camera, and her clothing elevate her as a figure of authority over these new parents.

From the tone and content of this advertisement, it's clear who knows more about parenting. The visitor not only has the education to understand parenting, but she also has the state-funded technology. She has the plan for the baby's life. The parents are submissive to her because they understand that things will go best for the baby if they're "involved" but not "in charge."

Is this assumption really true? Does the "expert" know what's best for your child? Does she have children? Is she raising her children the way you want to raise yours? Does she know that your child started sitting up at 5 months and that he's allergic to soy? Does she know that he responds especially well to music but hates car rides? Does she know that his father had dyslexia? Of course she doesn't; how could she? It's not that the expert is deficient in any way. She's just not his mother, so there are a million things she doesn't know about this child. And yet, because of credentials offered to her, she assumes a position of authority over fellow citizens.

Let's call this boy Henry. Here he is again with his obviously loving mother. NElovesPS reminds us that "Parents are one of the most critical factors." They don't want parents to feel cut out of the equation completely (that's currently against the law), but they do want to remind parents that they're not the *only* factor. It's a little unclear from this ad what the factors are about. Are we talking about factors of academic success? Factors of pliability? Factors of conformity to the current education system? Not sure.

But one message from this ad is clear: if you're a loving mother like Henry's, you'll get on board with the whole Nebraska early childhood plan. It's a clever way to extend power and influence. If the public school system waits to start educating children until they're 5 or 6 years old, the system will have missed out on a lot of opportunity. Some of the kids' ideas and habits will already be formed by kindergarten. Also, they'll miss out on a lot of money and political power. This may sound overly cynical, but ad campaigns like this one, which attempt to nudge parents away from their sacred duties to raise their children, deserve extreme skepticism.

It's worth noting that NElovesPS is funded by the Sherwood Foundation, Susan Buffett's organization that "promotes equity through social justice initiatives enhancing the quality of life in Nebraska," according to their website.[12] And the Buffett Early Childhood Institute is "working to develop a comprehensive plan for expanding and strengthening the state's early childhood workforce." What better way to create more jobs in early childhood education than to hire people like the lady who goes into people's homes to tell them how to raise their children?

Campaigns like this, which seem designed to gently steer parents away from their instinctive roles and responsibilities, warrant critical examination. Ultimately, parents, as the primary caregivers and advocates for their children, must remain central, respected figures in any narrative about child-rearing and education.

## Summary

- Birth practices teach parents to "trust the experts."
- The experts often have conflicts of interest.
- Districts aren't structured to see children as individuals.
- Practice reading the rhetoric: Nebraska Loves Public Schools Twitter/X Campaign.

**Go Deeper**

Mendelsohn, Robert S. *Male Practice: How Doctors Manipulate Women*. Chicago: Contemporary Books, Inc., 198.

In this book, author Robert S. Mendelsohn, a physician himself, provides a critical examination of the medical profession's treatment of female patients. The mistreatment is framed as sexism, but in my experience, female doctors are just as likely to dismiss parental concerns and push unnecessary therapeutics on patients as male doctors. The book explores a wide range of issues related to women's health, including patronizing attitudes, childbirth, abortion, and over-treatment of hysterectomy and other surgeries. Mendelsohn calls for a reevaluation of medical practices to promote a more respectful and egalitarian relationship between doctors and their female patients. Although Mendelsohn doesn't talk about K-12 education in this book, the parallels are unmistakable. If you can learn to deal with healthcare, you can deal with education.

# Chapter 3

# Taking the Reins

Clearly, too many other people have ideas about what your child can do for them. Your child in a public school seat counts for about $15,000 per year. Your child showing up for well-child visits ensures a steady stream of income supporting your pediatrician's office. Your child showing up at Drag Queen Story Hour increases the likelihood that the Marxists will have another recruit who will spout their ideology.

But what if you have other ideas about your child's upbringing? What if you don't want your child co-opted by those who turn children into dollar signs and uncritical voters?

You can take the reins begins with focusing on three things:

- **Principle #1:** Protection
- **Principle #2:** Preparation
- **Principle #3:** Paideia

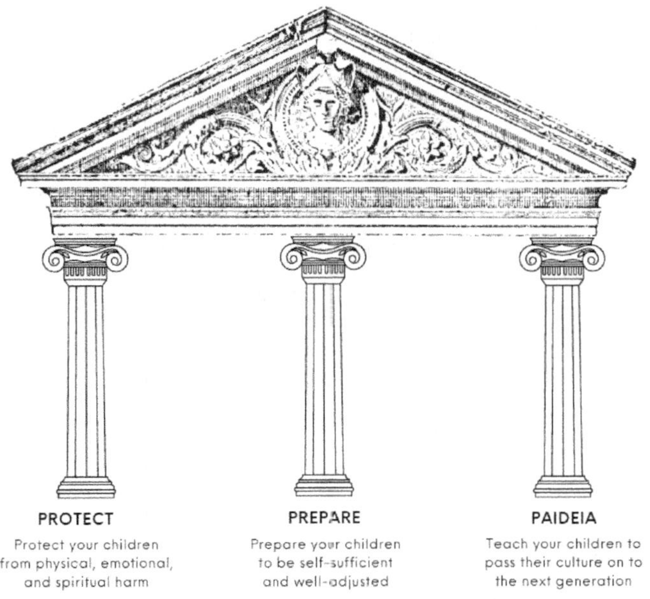


Most of us are familiar with the first two principles, and soon, you'll also understand paideia and hopefully see its significance for your children's future.

In the rest of this book, we'll explore all three principles in depth. Here, I'll just provide a brief overview of each one.

## Principle #1: Protection

Earlier in the book, I told the story of Nikki Bradshaw Carpenter, the young mother who piled pillows on top of her three sons and protected them with her own body. Protecting our children physically is an essential role for parents.

When newborns arrive, they're completely, utterly dependent on their parents for day-to-day survival. My newborns struggled even to get their own thumbs in their mouths for a little comfort. As children grow, they become more and more physically independent, learning to feed themselves, walk, and speak. Children face many physical dangers, and parents are generally confident in their abilities to keep their children from running into the street or drowning in a pool. Fortunately for us, the world is physically safer for children than it has been for many other generations. Between 1990 and 2013, child mortality rates fell by nearly half. And between 1997 and 2015, reports of missing children fell by 40 percent.[13] Kids are even less likely to be hit by a car today than they were in 1990. Better pedestrian infrastructure and safety standards for cars may play roles in these improvements. Whatever the reason, kids have a better chance of growing up without serious accidents than in the past, and this is terrific news.

When it comes to education, physical protection is not the primary concern (although we'll cover bullying and sexual abuse later on). Instead, our kids face academic, mental, and emotional peril.

In their book *Stolen Youth*, Bethany Mandel and Karol Markowicz argue that certain political ideologies have profoundly impacted childhood, encroaching upon a precious period of innocence that is vital for healthy human development. Much of this influence, they contend, comes from K-12 government schools. In the past, students with modest or mediocre academic beginnings still enjoyed a healthy childhood, supported by mentors who protected their innocence.

In contrast, today's children face new stressors, as adult worries and political agendas increasingly pervade their lives. This imposition deprives children of the freedom and space to engage in imaginative play and explore their world organically. For instance, researchers at Imperial College London found that 'eco-anxiety'—stress related to environmental concerns—affects more than 45% of young people surveyed across ten countries, impinging on their daily lives. In the U.S., some school districts have extended comprehensive sex education to include kindergarteners, a move that has stirred considerable debate, as reflected in media headlines like this one from NPR: "The Case for Starting Sex Ed in Kindergarten (Hula Hoops Recommended)."[14]

So if you're a parent who believes in romance, traditional families, morality, and childhood, you have some serious protecting to do.

## Principle #2: Prepare

Training students to adopt Marxist ideology takes time, and the school day has not significantly increased in recent generations. As a result, government schools may not be devoting as much time to core academics as they once did, potentially leaving students less prepared for the future.

Consider the exam questions that occasionally circulate on social media, such as these excerpts from a 1912 eighth-grade graduation exam in Bullitt County, Kentucky.

### *Arithmetic*

- Find the amount of $50.30 for 3 years, 3 months, and 3 days at 8 per cent.
- How many steps 2 ft. 4 in. each will a man take in walking 2 1/4 miles?
- At $1.62 1/2 a cord, what will be the cost of a pile of wood 24 ft. long, 4 ft. wide and 6 ft. 3 in. high?

### *Grammar*

- How many parts of speech are there? Define each.
- Adjectives have how many Degrees of Comparison? Compare good; wise; beautiful.

- Diagram: The Lord loveth a cheerful giver.

### *Geography*

- Name and give boundaries of the five zones.
- Locate the following countries which border each other: Turkey, Greece, Servia, Montenegro, Romania.
- Locate the following mountains: Blue Ridge, Himalaya, Andes, Alps, Wasatch.

### *Physiology*

- How does the liver compare in size with other glands in the human body? Where is it located? What does it secrete?
- Compare arteries and veins as to function. Where is the blood carried to be purified?
- Define Cerebrum; Cerebellum.

### *Civil Government*

- Define the following forms of government: Democracy, Limited Monarchy, Absolute Monarchy, Republic. Give examples of each.
- Name five county officers, and the principal duties of each.
- Name three rights given Congress by the Constitution and two rights denied Congress.

### *History*

- During what wars were the following battles fought:—Brandywine, Great Meadows, Lundy's Lane, Antietam, Buena Vista.
- Name 2 presidents who have died in office: three who were assassinated.
- Who invented the following.—Magnetic, Telegraph, Cotton Gin, Sewing Machine, Telephone, Phonograph.

*Smithsonian Magazine* reprinted this exam in its entirety, noting that it reflects "outdated ideas of education"—so there's no need to feel bad if you can't pass it.[15] But it prompts us to ask: Why is it outdated to understand the world's geography or the mechanics of government? Shouldn't we know the grammar of the language we use every day?

The 2020 school shutdowns served as a wake-up call for many parents who had previously assumed that all was well within school walls. The transition to virtual classes, or 'Zoom school,' pulled back the curtain, allowing parents across the country to see firsthand what their children were learning—and not learning. Tiffany Justice, co-founder of Moms for Liberty, poignantly observed: "What we learned is that our children's education is being stolen from them and replaced with ideological narratives that aren't nurturing their full potential in life."[16]

In response, homeschooling rates have surged. Parents began exploring curricula and learning materials, perhaps for the first time, and many came to realize that they themselves missed out on a quality education. The decline in American K-12 education, unfortunately, has been unfolding for generations.

This is why it's crucial for parents to step up—and it's no small task. The goal isn't merely to restore what might have been lost in recent years, nor is it about giving your children the education that you had, especially if your own education was lacking in certain areas. Instead, the aspiration is even more ambitious: to provide this generation of children with an education that is superior to our own.

It's time to ignite a renaissance of learning in the United States—and this call to action extends to other Western nations as well.

## Principle #3: Paideia

Pronounce it "py-day-a."

If this word seems entirely unfamiliar, you're in good company. Its use has waned over the past few generations, but fortunately, we are witnessing a revival of both the word "paideia" and the philosophy it represents.

Derived from the Greek word "pais" or "paidos," "paideia" initially referred to the upbringing of a child, echoing today's "pedagogy" and "pediatrics." However, its meaning evolved to encompass a broader concept: the general learning and education accessible to all individuals. This is similar to the Latin term "humanitas," from which we get the "humanities." Paideia was fundamental to the Greek educational system, leaving an enduring legacy on subsequent ages through its role in shaping Greek character.

In classical Greek tradition, paideia represented a comprehensive system of education aimed at nurturing well-rounded and enlightened citizens. This holistic curriculum included subjects ranging from gymnastics, grammar, and rhetoric to poetry, music, mathematics, and philosophy. The goal was to cultivate individuals endowed with both intellectual and moral virtues, equipping them to contribute significantly to society.

Civilization, tradition, literature, culture, and education are all interconnected facets of paideia. It targeted the development of an elevated human character—the Greeks were renowned for their unique alignment with the universal laws of human nature. They established a standard of humanity that served as a touchstone for educators, poets, artists, and philosophers alike.

To summarize, paideia originated from the Greek concept of upbringing but evolved to signify a robust system of education and training. It endeavored to nurture individuals who were balanced in intellectual and moral virtues and who embodied an ideal of humanity. Paideia guided young Greeks in understanding their civilization and helped shape them into productive, ethical citizens who would, in turn, pass their culture on to future generations.

In fact, without the flourishing of Ancient Greek culture—fostered by their educational standards and methods—Western civilization, including America, might appear markedly different today. Sadly, there are signs that Western civilization is in decline, visible everywhere from uninspired art and architecture to a pervasive lack of honesty and integrity.

But here lies an important opportunity for parents: the way we raise our children can significantly impact the future. Adopting a paideia mindset involves more than making sure our children can add, subtract, or write a five-paragraph essay. It means actively passing our culture to the next generation, instilling values of beauty, truth, family, and the rich heritage we've inherited from our ancestors.

## Protect, Prepare, Paideia

This book focuses on three key principles. We begin with Protection, emphasizing the importance of safeguarding children and providing them with a secure environment in which to grow during their formative years.

We then move on to Preparation, where we explore the critical role of education. Our goal is to ensure children receive not just adequate schooling, but truly exceptional learning experiences that foster a comprehensive understanding of the world throughout their K-12 education.

Finally, we address the concept of Paideia. If our culture has a chance of surviving the current onslaught, we must teach our children to honor and respect the heritage they've inherited. We examine historical patterns that reveal how authoritarian regimes often attempt to erase existing cultural foundations, and we consider the implications of this phenomenon. We've seen this with the Bolsheviks, the Soviets, the Chinese Communist Party, and North Korea. All of these governments attempted to erase their people's existing culture. In China, the Red Guards worked to destroy the Four Olds (old ideas, old customs, old culture, and old habits). They accomplished their work by destroying historical artifacts and religious and cultural sites. Additionally, they targeted people who represented the Four Olds. Alarmingly, we are witnessing attempts to replicate this pattern in the United States and across the Western world. Marxist activists throw paint at treasured works of art, tear down statues, and burn churches. These are obvious, outward attempts to destroy the past. But their most effective way to change the culture and erase the past is to control the education system.

Fortunately, when parents genuinely embrace their responsibilities toward their children's upbringing and education, these authoritarian influences can be effectively countered. The power to shape the next generation lies firmly in our hands. With fortitude and a little know-how, parents can loosen the grip that oppressive forces try to exert on our young.

We, as parents and guardians, are not only up for this task, we are committed to it. It is up to us to champion these principles and lead the way toward a brighter, more secure future for our children.

## Summary

- Principle #1: Protect
- Principle #2: Prepare
- Principle #3: Paideia

### Go Deeper

If you have 12 minutes to spare right now, head over to YouTube and watch Rebekah Hagstrom's TEDxMahtomedi talk about classical education. Entitled "What if everyone had a classical education?" this talk explores the benefits of paideia. What happens when children know history, understand logic, and can speak and debate respectfully? Find Hagstrom's talk at this link: https://youtu.be/0m5yDZCy2pE

# Part I - Protect

# Chapter 4

# Cherish Childhood

Venugopal Acharya holds advanced degrees in monetary policy and economics and has worked with many multinational companies, but he has also served as a monk and spiritual teacher for over two decades. How does he describe childhood? "Childhood is the best of all the seasons of life, and the longer it lasts with happy memories, the stronger the emotional stability in adulthood." When you provide your child with a happy childhood, you build a strong, stable foundation for her future.

Childhood is a precious and magical time characterized by innocence, wonder, and boundless imagination. During this period, children possess a remarkable ability to perceive the world with a sense of awe and curiosity. They approach each day with an open mind, unburdened by the worries and responsibilities of adulthood.

As such, childhood is a time of intense growth and development, both physically and emotionally. It's when young minds absorb knowledge like sponges, soaking up information and experiences that shape their understanding of the world. Every interaction, every lesson, and every new discovery leaves an imprint on their minds, shaping their perspectives and forming the foundation of their future selves.

Furthermore, childhood should be a time of joy and laughter. Children find pleasure in the simplest things—a caterpillar, a cardboard box, or your silliest dad joke. Their ability to find wonder in the ordinary reminds us all to slow down and appreciate the beauty surrounding us. During this phase, lifelong friendships are formed, memories are created, and the seeds of happiness are sown.

Childhood is also a time of freedom and exploration. Children have the luxury of being blissfully unaware of the constraints and responsibilities that await them in adulthood. They can indulge in their passions, explore their interests, and pursue their dreams with abandon. It is a time when creativity knows no bounds and possibilities seem endless.

In a world that often demands too much from us, childhood remains a sanctuary. Parents should treasure and protect children's childhoods, allowing them to grow, learn, and flourish in a wholesome environment. Childhood experiences shape adult identity, underscoring the importance of cherishing this brief, formative period.

However, some people want to hijack childhood. Since children are so impressionable, it's the perfect time to shape their perceptions of the world. And all too often, people who want to control others aim to make children believe in things that are contrary to what they see before their eyes.

In the image below, you'll see the three pillars introduced earlier in the book—protection, preparation, and paideia. They provide the foundation for a healthy, productive childhood. As you can see, the children in the image are protected from harmful influences. I'm not suggesting that you can make sure your children never encounter pornography or propaganda, but you can significantly reduce their influence.

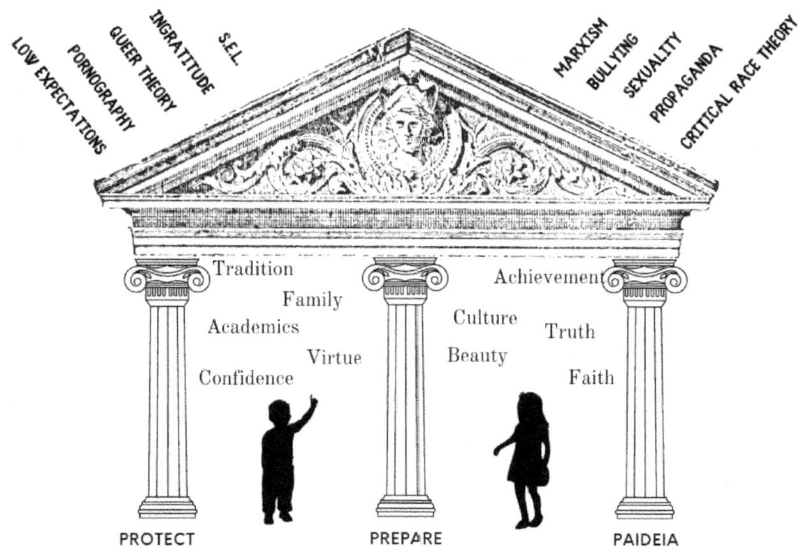


At the same time, the three P's provide space for the good things in life: faith, family, beauty, truth, and more. We're not just trying to avoid bad influences; we want to fill children's lives with the noble and beautiful.

How serious are the threats to childhood today? The following transcripts come from TikTok. The first two are videos produced by public school teachers, and the third is a flyer for an event at an elementary school.

### 1. Middle School Teacher: "conversations I have about queerness and transness with my kids"

*So the conversation I talked about in my last video is a lot like a lot of the conversations I have about queerness and transness with my kids. Um, because I work in a conservative area, and I'm an out non-binary trans teacher, I have to tread very lightly for fear of losing my job. And so, a lot of times I put it in terms of hypotheticals with the kids. I say, "Oh, some people like to use this, when I talk about my title "Mx." I say, "Oh, it's just a third alternative to Mr., Ms., that some people like to use." I let them kind of draw their own conclusions when it comes back to me while also keeping it kind of general enough to not bring the heat on myself.*

*@hound_oflove*

This teacher claims to be concerned about losing her job if word gets out about her views on transgenderism, but she posted this video to TikTok, so she couldn't have been too worried. Public school teachers know that their postmodern views will very rarely get them in trouble.

She sounds like she doesn't want to come right out and tell them to call her "Mx. So-and-so," but she does make it all about her. In all my years growing up, I don't remember teachers talking about themselves to this extent.

And no, "Mx" is not an alternative to Mr. and Ms. and Mrs. It's completely made up and has no place in a school. Worse than the affront to language is the offense against Truth. Humans are male or female, and teaching otherwise is simply teaching lies to innocents.

### 2. Elementary School Teacher: they know that I identify as neither

*So I had an interesting conversation with my students the other day because we were talking about the Civil Rights Movement. Um and if you're someone who doesn't agree with like kids learning about transgender people, please just scroll and keep your negativity to yourself. So we were comparing the civil rights movement to um civil rights that are being fought for today and comparing how people are fighting for these things. Of course, we compared um issues coming up with race cause that is most directly connected to the Civil Rights Movement, but in a video I shared they discuss that civil rights are being fought for many different types of people to make sure everyone has the same rights. They mentioned fighting for rights for people of color, for women, for immigrants, and lastly, they said gay, lesbian, and transgender people. Now, many of my students already know about gay and lesbian people um, but they didn't understand what transgender meant. Now, with my students being second graders, I had to make sure that my um lesson was um appropriate for that age group. I simply said that a transgender person is born um in a boy or girl body and then in their heart they know that that doesn't match who they are and so they might then identify by a different gender. It might be a boy who identifies as a girl, a girl who identifies as a boy. Apologies for having to change the venue [there was an interruption in her recording]. But lastly, I explained that it could be a boy that's a girl, a girl that's a boy, or someone who feels like neither. Now, why I felt okay sharing this was because I, they know that I identify as neither. I go by Mx. and not Mr. or Miss. Also, I told them about the trans teacher that teaches 3rd grade. They are male to female uh transgender. But the funniest thing happened when I was explaining, you know, I don't really feel like a girl, but I know I definitely am not a boy, so you know I consider myself non-binary, which means, you know, neither. And so someone's like, "so does that mean you're mixed?" [laughter] And I like that they understand these terms because they understand that if someone is, you know, two different races that they're mixed. So because I was neither they're like, "so you're in the middle. That means you're mixed." [laughter] And I was like, you know, if that helps you understand it that is perfect. Yes, I'm mixed. So I will no longer be identifying as non-binary. I will simply be identifying as mixed.*

*@theone.n.onlyzoe*

First of all, comparing transgenderism to race is ridiculous. Your race is an immutable characteristic. You can't change it. And certainly, people should never judge each other based on immutable characteristics.

On the other hand, transgenderism is based on the very idea that you can change immutable characteristics. Your gender is something you're born with. You can't change it, no matter how many surgeries you have. Your very cells speak your gender. And yet, this woman is teaching 7-year-olds that they can in fact change their gender and that people who attempt to do so are like a race of people.

Again, why are teachers talking with their students about their personal problems? When did this narcissism become acceptable?

### *3. Atkinson Elementary School (Portland Public Schools) PRIDE FEST flyer*

*ATK GSA Presents*

*PRIDE FEST - May 19th, 2023*

*3pm - Settling into the space with queens greeting folk*

*3:20pm - Lala's official welcome and introductions*

*4pm - Overview of the space and activities available*

*4:05-5:00pm - Activity stations open to all including Drag Queen Story Time, makeup station, nail polish station, craft station, tarot station, self-defense demo presentation, & clothing swap station*

*4-4:30 - Gender affirming Q&A for Atkinson adults with Miss Madi and Elliott Hinkle of Unicorn Solutions*

*5pm - Closing*

Why are the adults in the Portland Public Schools keen on putting make-up on elementary students? And a tarot station at a school festival? Childhood is a precious time, and adults must it. An elementary school fair should be a family-friendly event with cakewalks, music, and child-centric games. Somehow, activists have weaseled their way into these events and made a traditional community event into a narcissistic exhibition.

Even if you're not seeing such blatant attacks on childhood in your area, it seems that adult ideologues are chipping away at innocence from every possible angle.

## The library

Maria Martin wants her preschoolers to have the kind of childhood she had. She loved reading, "In an old house in Paris that was covered with vines, lived 12 little girls in two straight lines" (*Madeline*). And don't forget:

"Mr Knox, sir
Let's do tricks with
Bricks and blocks, sir
Let's do tricks with
Chicks and clocks, sir"
(*Fox in Socks*)

But when Maria takes her kids to the local library today, the books on display aren't the innocent storybooks of her childhood. Sure, you can find Dr. Seuss and Ludwig Bemelmans in the stacks. But the ones featured front and center have titles like, *A is for Activist* and *Kamala Harris: Rooted in Justice*.

Maria pays her taxes, which purchase the books for the library. So she patiently rearranges the book displays, replacing Ruth Bader Ginsberg biographies with Robert Louis Stevenson's poetry. Her children deserve to read about imagining themselves to be pirates just as much as other generations of children. Why should their childhoods be dominated by Marxist indoctrination?

In Maria's view, she is not just preserving classic literature; she is safeguarding her children's right to an innocent and joyful childhood. She finds herself questioning why their formative years should be influenced by political agendas and ideological propaganda, rather than the timeless joy of imagination unbound.

In a small, conservative town, Kyra checked out one of the activity boxes at her local library. These themed plastic totes included books, toys, and other activities that families could take home and enjoy. Originally from Hawaii, Kyra thought it would be fun to check out the Hawaii activity box. When she got home and her kids started rifling through the box (which was zip-tied at the library so she couldn't see what was inside), Kyra was shocked to find a book about a young Hawaiian girl who felt like she might be a boy. Kyra wasn't the only parent who was dismayed about this book being included in the Hawaii activity box. Another parent met with one of the librarians who informed her that transgenderism was part of Hawaii's traditional culture. Of course this is nonsense, and when Kyra told her Hawaiian family about this assertion, they were shocked. But in academia, scholars have been tying LGBT priorities to indigenous people for years. For example, in 2014, Gregory D. Smithers, professor of history at Virginia Commonwealth University, published an article about Cherokee "two spirits" were inhabited by both male and female spirits, providing back-up for today's gender activists. Smithers isn't alone. According to U.S. News and World Report, there are over 400 gender studies programs at universities in the United States. These programs churn out activists year after year. Of course they're going to produce propaganda for children.

But you don't have to go to the library to find media that robs your children of their innocence. It gets piped right into your home.

## Media that steals childhood

Education begins long before the first day of preschool. In fact, learning begins when life begins. Therefore, everything you expose your children to teaches them something about the way the world works.

A recent episode of *Transformers: EarthSpark* included the following conversation between a human girl and two robots:

**1st Robot:** My pronouns are they/them.

**Girl:** Thanks. I'm Sam. I'm she/they. But you already know that.

**2nd Robot:** Wow, what an amazing city!

**Girl:** I'm sorry for how I reacted. It's just sometimes the world can be a scary place. It's hard to know who's dangerous or not.

**2nd Robot:** hmm. That's true, though disappointing.

**Girl:** Hey, it's okay. I know I'm safe when I'm with my friends or other non-binary people.

**2nd Robot:** Non-binary?

**Girl:** People who aren't female or male. Oh, I'm sorry. I shouldn't have assumed.

**2nd Robot:** I always knew my pronouns felt right, but what a wonderful word for a wonderful experience.

It wouldn't be surprising for kids to understand from this show that non-binary people are "the good guys" and everyone else is scary. Also, it's teaching children to talk about pronouns the way Mr. Rogers used to teach children to say "please" and "thank you." Even a few episodes of a show like this could cause serious confusion in young children.

Gone are the days when parents could let their children turn on the TV to watch cartoons without a second thought about the content. In today's media landscape, a proactive approach is necessary for parents who want to preserve the innocence of their children's formative years and foster a love for beauty and truth.

One effective strategy is to minimize screen time. Instead of daily, casual screen time, consider reserving it for special family movie nights. Make these occasions memorable and enjoyable, complete with popcorn and treats. Watch films and shows together as a family, allowing for opportunities to discuss anything that might be confusing or questionable. It's also a chance to revisit the vast collection of high-quality children's programming from past decades, which can be both entertaining and wholesome.

Fortunately, initiatives are emerging to address this concern. For instance, Daily Wire and similar organizations are actively working to create new, engaging content for children that steers clear of heavy ideological messages or inappropriate themes. By supporting these efforts through viewership or subscription, parents can contribute to a growing demand for such content, encouraging the production of more options that align with these values.

In this evolving media landscape, parents are more than consumers; they are stewards of their children's mental and emotional landscapes. It's a responsibility that comes with challenges, but also with the unparalleled reward of nurturing a generation attuned to beauty, truth, and meaningful storytelling.

## Let kids be kids

When the airplanes struck the World Trade Center on September 11, 2001, I had a baby and a toddler at home. Consumed with worry, I was tempted to keep the TV on all day long, but one look into my 3-year-old's eyes as she saw the chaotic scene playing out on the screen made me realize that it would be irresponsible to keep the TV on. Young children can't grasp that each replay of a single tragic event is not a new occurrence. Nor do they have the mental tools to understand distance, risk factors, and the intricate nature of our world.

Life naturally presents challenges to children, just as it does to adults. Kids experience sickness, injury, conflicts with friends and siblings, and sometimes even more substantial hardships like disability, death, and family divorce. These difficulties are already substantial burdens for them to navigate. We all grow through trials, but that doesn't mean we need to add unnecessary worries onto children's shoulders.

So, what kinds of concerns should we avoid placing on them?

### *Environmental Catastrophizing*

A multi-country research study found that 59 percent of children and young people were very or extremely worried about climate change, with 84 percent at least moderately concerned. This "eco-anxiety" manifests as worry, fear, anger, grief, despair, guilt, and shame. Instead of instilling fear over issues largely beyond their control, we should encourage children to be good stewards of the environment and celebrate their efforts. Teach them tangible, positive actions, such as cleaning up after a picnic in the park, planting vegetables, or composting.

### *Adult Sexuality*

Social media platforms, like TikTok, are increasingly exposing children to conversations about adult sexual identities. While educators have a right to their personal lives, it is inappropriate to seek personal affirmation from students. The classroom should remain a place focused on education and mentorship, not the personal lives of the adults in charge.

### *Global Politics and Conflicts*

Children are not mini adults; they do not need to be informed about every geopolitical conflict or political strife happening around the world. While teaching them to be compassionate and aware of different cultures is important, burdening them with the complexities of war, terrorism, or political unrest can create unnecessary and un-useful anxiety.

### *Health Concerns*

Kids should be taught the importance of good health and hygiene, but they don't need to know the intricate details of a relative's severe medical condition or the potential health hazards in the world. It's important to strike a balance between awareness and undue stress.

### *Social Identity Conflicts*

Avoid placing adult concepts of cultural, racial, or social identity politics on children. Encourage a love for and curiosity about different people without instilling a sense of guilt or conflict about their own identity.

## Creating child-friendly communities

In today's climate, it can be a challenge to find like-minded families who share your values, especially when it comes to preserving the innocence of childhood. Seek connections with other parents who are working towards the same goal. These families can be invaluable, not only as a social resource but also as potential partners in education.

Such networks can empower parents to create enriching, high-quality educational environments, whether that's through homeschooling, micro-schooling, or simply staying informed about what is happening in their children's schools.

## Finding Your Tribe

To connect with these families, consider:

- Becoming involved with your local church or faith community
- Engaging in conversations with friends and neighbors about children and parenting
- Joining a homeschool co-op, if you are homeschooling
- Attending school board meetings and connecting with like-minded parents

Remember, you are not alone in this endeavor. If you feel isolated, it's likely because you haven't found your community yet. But rest assured—they are out there, and they are hoping to find you too. Dr. Jonathan Haidt has been on a mission in recent years to help parents understand the dangers of smartphones.[17] He has called on school administrators to raise the bar by keeping phones out the classroom. Recognizing that kids can feel isolated if they perceive themselves to be the only ones without phones, Haidt encourages parents to coordinate with the parents of their children's friends to create phone-free havens. When none of the kids in a friend group have smartphones, no one feels left out.

So, reach out, engage, and start building a network of parents dedicated to safeguarding the joyful, innocent years of childhood. Look for organizations like Smartphone Free Childhood to find people in your local community who are seeking to protect kids' childhoods. Together, you can significantly enhance your family's quality of life.

## Summary

- From schoolteachers to media, many people are trying to force Marxist ideology on children.
- Some media can rob children of their innocence and force harmful or scary ideas on them too soon.
- You can take intentional steps to create a carefree childhood for your kids.
- Create relationships with other families who let kids be kids.

### Go Deeper

Mandel, Bethany, and Karol Markowicz. *Stolen Youth: How Radicals Are Erasing Innocence and Indoctrinating a Generation*. DW Books, 2023.

In an interview about the book *Stolen Youth*, Karol Markowicz relays an experience about her little boy. "In the book, I tell the story of allowing my then-1st grader, my middle child, to march in his school's climate march. We had moved within Brooklyn and he had transferred schools after the school year had begun. I didn't want him to sit it out and stick out. That was a huge mistake. I would absolutely never allow my kids to be used for any political purpose. No UNICEF collecting on Halloween, no "anti-hate" marches like schools in Brooklyn have done, nothing. It requires bravery, yes, but ultimately not that much. Your kid will feel weird for one day, but they'll learn a lesson about standing up for their values. But bigger picture, join with other parents to stop this ridiculous spectacle from happening in the first place."[19]

# Chapter 5

# Where Do Kids Spend Their Time?

In 2022, three Pennsylvania mothers filed a lawsuit against their children's first grade teacher for teaching their 6- and 7-year-olds about gender transitioning without their consent. According to the lawsuit, the teacher, Megan Williams, had gone as far as telling her young students that "parents are wrong" and parents and doctors "make mistakes" when they bring a child home from the hospital and say that he or she is a boy or a girl.[20]

Not only do some educators teach philosophies that are at odds with parents' value systems (and the truth), but they feel they have a right to do this because of their credentials. Special education public school teacher Alicia Messing testified in front of an Arizona state Senate Education Committee against parents having a say in the curriculum used to teach their children.

She said, "I have a Master's degree, because when I got certified, I was told I had to have a Master's degree to be an Arizona-certified teacher. We all have advanced degrees. What do the parents have? Are we vetting the backgrounds of our parents? Are we allowing the parents to choose the curriculum and the books that our children are going to read? I think that it's a mistake—and I'm just speaking from the heart—the one line that I love is, 'we must remember that the purpose of public education is not to teach only what parents want their children to be taught, it is to teach them what society needs them to be taught.'"

Messing is not alone in her opinion that teachers, not parents, should be in the driver's seat for all children in our society. After facing criticism for exposing children to media that parents found objectionable,[21] Florida teacher Jenna Barbee went on CNN and said that "rights as a parent, those rights are gone when your child is in the public school system."[22] Of course this isn't true. Where have educators gotten the idea that they have a right (and even a responsibility) to go against parents' wishes and do what they want with children?

From school board meetings to social media, conversations on this topic often veer toward the fact that teachers are specially trained experts in children's education. But even if we had decent teacher certification processes in this country, which we don't, parents are still the best people to make educational decisions for their children. After all, they know their children better than anyone else.

## Where do your kids spend time?

Children should be in school. That's a statement that few people in the United States would argue with. After all, gone are the days when children had to work in the fields or the mines for survival. Today's children have the benefit of spending their days in learning institutions where they prepare for productive adulthood.

That's what they say. But are your kids protected from degeneracy, apathy, and Marxist ideologies at school?

I learned this lesson in dramatic fashion—delivered as a lawsuit threat. Here's how it went down.

I picked our $6^{th}$ and $8^{th}$ graders up from school every afternoon. One day, I could tell that something was wrong before the kids even got to the car. For one thing, my $8^{th}$ grade son had his arm around his $6^{th}$ grade sister. That wasn't normal. She had tears in her eyes, and he looked angry. I started to get out of the car to find out what was wrong, expecting to hear about an injury.

They both started talking at once, and my daughter bit her lip. She was holding back tears.

"One at a time," I said.

"We had an assembly," my daughter began.

"I can't believe they would talk about that stuff at an assembly!" My son said. "They're $6^{th}$ graders!"

"What was the assembly about?" I asked.

Words came tumbling out. I couldn't understand exactly what happened at the assembly, but I could understand that there was bad language and talk about sex and she had felt very uncomfortable. I needed more information before I could know how to handle it, so I went home and emailed the principal.

She responded quickly, but I was stunned by what I read. I had assumed I would get some detailed clarification that would help me to talk through it with my daughter. She was 11, after all, and she probably had misunderstood things.

But the principal just said, "I'm sorry your daughter felt uncomfortable."

*Beg your pardon?*

My daughter is in tears over something presented to her by adults at school, and all I get is, "I'm sorry your daughter felt uncomfortable"?

I asked for more information, and she wouldn't give me any, so I asked some of my daughters' teachers if they could elaborate.

Her homeroom teacher told me that it was as bad as she'd said. He said he felt terrible through the whole thing and couldn't believe they'd show such things to kids.

I asked the principal if I could watch a video of the program. She said they didn't have video, but she could put me in touch with the woman who created the program. Her name was Sue Letheby.

I emailed Letheby and asked for more information about the program. She told me I could come watch it when they performed it at another school, or I could have a copy of the script. I asked for the script.

It was far more sexual than I thought an 11-year-old should be hearing about, although I didn't read any swear words. I asked the homeroom teacher, and he thought they'd thrown in some swear words that weren't in the script.

Since Letheby assured me that no one had ever complained before and that it was a district-wide program, I wrote to the district to express my concerns. I thought maybe I could spare some kids in the future.

On the day before Thanksgiving, the doorbell rang. It was a courier with a legal-size envelope I had to sign for. I looked at the return address and was surprised to see the name and address of a law firm.

I was a stay-at-home mom taking a break from making Thanksgiving dinner to answer the door, and I was being served papers for a defamation lawsuit. By whom? By Sue Letheby, the creator of the assembly that had made my daughter cry at school.

My face flushed hot, and my heart started pounding. I read the letter through a couple of times to try to understand what was happening. She was demanding that I apologize and retract my statement to the district saying that the assembly was inappropriate for sixth graders.

I started to see that I was an obstacle to these educators. They knew what was best for my children, and I ought to defer to their expertise. And if I didn't, well, I would have to pay the price.

Friends connected me with a local attorney who not only quashed any legal action from Sue Letheby. He also gave me the confidence to stick to my intuition.

His letter back to Letheby's attorney began like this:

> *I represent Rachel Terry who is in receipt of your November 25, 2014, letter. In 24 years of practice, this is the most ironic letter I have ever had the pleasure of reading: a bullying letter sent on behalf of an alleged anti-bullying advocate.*
>
> *There has been no defamation here: Rachel Terry truthfully and accurately relayed her 11-year-old daughter's perceptions to school officials after her daughter was (rightly) disturbed by a play that contained references like "fag," "faggot," "hook up," "let's have sex," "spread her legs," "slut," and "Irish whore."*
>
> *Enclosed is a copy of the script that Ms. Letheby provided to Rachel Terry. Your letter states that Rachel Terry made "false and defamatory statements" when she described the contents of the play as containing profanity and sexual innuendo. Since truth is an absolute defense to a defamation claim, the script should provide you all the information that you will need to advise your client that she has no case.*

I never heard from Susan Letheby or her attorney again. This was nearly a decade ago, and we all know that the environment at public schools has only degenerated since then. From drag queens to Planned Parenthood guest speakers, adults with their own agendas regularly "teach" innocent children during the hours they're away from their parents. Constant vigilance is imperative.

## Friends' homes

As parents, we are responsible for creating a supportive environment that nurtures our children's social interactions and friendships. Part of this responsibility involves understanding the significance of knowing what's going on at your children's friends' homes. In this section, we will explore why this knowledge is important and how it influences your child's growth.

By being aware of what's happening at your children's friends' homes, you can assess the environments they are exposed to. This knowledge allows you to identify any potential risks or dangers, ensuring that your child is in a safe and secure environment. By understanding the conditions and level of supervision in their friends' homes, you can make informed decisions about where your child spends his time.

Children are highly influenced by their surroundings and the people they interact with. Knowing what's happening at your children's friends' homes provides insights into the values, behaviors, and attitudes prevalent in those environments. This awareness enables you to assess whether these other environments align with your family's values and determine the impact they may have on your child. Understanding the dynamics of their friends' homes allows you to make informed decisions about the friendships your children developsand the influences they are exposed to.

Peer pressure is a significant factor during childhood and adolescence. By being knowledgeable about your children's friends' homes, you gain insights into the dynamics of those friendships. This understanding helps you identify any negative peer pressure that your child may be facing. Armed with this information, you can engage in open and honest conversations with your children about making responsible choices and equip them with strategies to handle peer pressure effectively.

## Activities / Coaches

Extracurricular activities present a fantastic opportunity for children to explore interests, develop friendships, stay physically active, and create enduring memories. However, parents must be mindful of the environments where their children are spending time and the individuals they are interacting with.

Consider an incident in Tennessee: a well-liked soccer coach inadvertently left his phone at a fast-food restaurant. Restaurant workers, attempting to identify the phone's owner, discovered disturbing content that led them to contact the police. This 63-year-old coach, a long-time resident of the area, had been visiting school playgrounds to recruit young players for his soccer team. According to police reports, he gained the trust of the children and their families, eventually inviting these young players to his home where unthinkable abuses occurred.[23]

In a different context, a summer camp leader known as Mx. Russo shared on TikTok how he trained the camp's children to run to him whenever he played a certain tune on his recorder. "I have so much power, and I love it," Russo said. "It's the perfect time to teach them about trans."

These stories illustrate the unsettling reality that individuals like Campos and Russo can build trust with both parents and children for their own purposes. These scenarios serve as stark reminders that while most coaches, teachers, and mentors are guided by positive motivations and ideals, there are exceptions.

Is there anything parents can do to protect their children from these rare but dangerous situations? Absolutely, yes.

First, it's about active engagement. Parents can attend practices or sessions when possible and get to know the adults who are interacting with their children. Ask questions. Who are these individuals? What are their backgrounds and qualifications? Are they appropriately vetted? Before signing your child up for music camp, check out the website and social media of the people who run it. Talk to other parents about options and help each other learn about the adults involved.

Second, keep communication open. Regular conversations with your children about their experiences in these activities provide insights. Are they comfortable? Do they feel safe? Have they noticed anything that makes them uneasy? One of my kids remembers a dinnertime conversation when my husband suggested that they be careful at their music practices because they were alone with an adult in a small practice room. She said she'd never thought about that before, but she knew then to be on the lookout for potential problems.

Third, create healthy boundaries between adults and children. If your child's coach wants to text your child, insist that you're copied on all communication or that all messages go directly to you. There's no reason for a teacher or coach to be able to communicate at all hours with your child. Additionally, there's no reason for kids to visit coach's homes or be in cars with them. An end-of-season party at a coach's house is safe, as long as parents are invited to attend.

Finally, trust your instincts. If something feels off, take it seriously. Don't be afraid to explore further and, if necessary, find alternative activities led by individuals whose values align with your family's.

Being proactive doesn't imply living in constant fear; rather, it's about being an engaged and discerning participant in your children's lives, creating a secure and enriching environment for them to grow and thrive.

## Give your children alignment

A major part of child development is learning to understand the world. Children must learn what's expected of them, how to successfully communicate with people, and what to do in various situations.

But when kids spend part of the day at a school where the rules, norms, and values are different than those of their homes, confusion ensues. Walter Blanks, Jr., a spokesperson for American Federation for Children, struggled at his district public school. He acted out and fell behind. Knowing his current path was unsustainable, Walter's parents pulled him out and enrolled him in a private school.

The private school held him back a grade so he could catch up. During that 6$^{th}$ grade year, he stayed in from recess and worked hard. He'd never been held to such high expectations at school before. But even at that young age, Walter noticed that he was finally at a school where the atmosphere aligned with his home life. "The private school I ended up going to, all of those things matched up: values, spirituality, academic rigor," he said. "And it was literally almost as if I was going to my second home every day. All of the teachers, all of the staff members—they were family."

Walter felt like he was home because the values and norms at his school aligned with the values and norms of his family. "My mom would often say, 'You're only going to get grades for the next 8 years, but then the rest of your life, you need to know how to be a strong person of convictions and values. I would much rather have you tell the truth every time than get an A on every test.'" Happily, not only did Walter grow into a strong person of convictions, but he also received an excellent education.

## Summary

- Be very aware of the environments where your children spend their time.
- Consider the atmosphere in friends' homes.
- Instill proper boundaries between your children and the adults in their lives.
- Provide your kids with alignment in the various places where they spend time.

### Go Deeper

Metaxas, Eric. *Bonhoeffer: Pastor, Martyr, Prophet, Spy*. Thomas Nelson, 1994.

Eric Metaxas's biography of Dietrich Bonhoeffer is not a quick, easy read. And you might be wondering why I recommend it as deeper reading for a chapter about where your kids spend their time. Well, it's this. Bonhoeffer's parents created a home where their children experienced love, faith, culture, education, beauty, and endless support. This foundation gave their son the conviction and confidence to stand against merciless forces as the Nazis clamped down on freedom and human rights. Ultimately, Dietrich Bonhoeffer helped orchestrate a plot to overthrow the Nazi regime. It's an incredible, inspiring story.

## Chapter 6

# Listening and Being There

On March 12, 2020, Virginia mother Merianne Jensen received news that her children would be leaving school early and wouldn't return for at least two weeks. "I sensed something was not right," she said. "It might have been a mother's intuition, but I could feel that my kids weren't going back to school anytime soon. At that moment, I knew I would have to start advocating for them."

Merianne's husband had studied viruses with an enthusiasm that most men reserve for fantasy football. He was confident that Covid-19 would not pose a threat to their family. The Jensens resolved that their children would not miss out on the education for which they, as taxpayers, were paying.

Remote schooling proved challenging for the Jensen kids. When the district eventually started transitioning back to in-person learning, the children were initially only allowed to attend school two days per week.

A few months later, Merianne had had enough. She firmly told the principal, "My children will be returning for four days a week. Figure it out; they will be coming back." When a principal resisted, Merianne's husband countered, "We're paying our tax dollars. Our children are entitled to this education. Make it work." The following Monday, the children resumed a four-day school week.

Emboldened by this small triumph, Merianne continued her advocacy. Initially, the Jensen children wore masks to school because of the mandates. But when Virginia elected a new governor, Merianne sensed an opportunity to challenge the mask mandate. She applied for a religious exemption, which, after two weeks, was approved. Nonetheless, school officials stipulated that her children must maintain six feet away from their classmates, sit behind plexiglass shields at their desks, and wear face shields during group work. Additionally, her son was instructed to walk at the back of the line.

Merianne spent hours discussing her concerns with school principals. She remained professional yet assertive. She'd ask, "Tell me how this makes sense. This is a religious exemption. The other children shouldn't even be aware of this exemption. Why should my children be treated differently?"

Merianne's persistence wasn't limited to private phone calls; she also voiced her perspective at a school board meeting. A clip of her speech went viral, inspiring parents nationwide to advocate for their children. She engaged with administrators at every turn. When the mask mandates were lifted, Merianne noticed that mask-enforcement signs still hung in the school's hallways. She visited the school, questioning the continued presence of the signs. When the school staff failed to take them down, she immediately called the superintendent. The signs were removed within half an hour.

Marianne's story demonstrates the significant impact one dedicated parent can make, not just for her own children, but for others who may feel that their rights are being overlooked. She serves as a powerful example of how steadfast advocacy can affect meaningful change.

You can't help if you don't know what's going on

Merianne Jensen knew what was going on and when to step in because she has always been an involved parent. Even before the Covid madness began, she showed up at her kids' schools often. She volunteered to serve as a room mother and shelved books at the library so she could see which books the library stocked.

In addition to spending time at the schools, she cultivated strong relationships with her children, so they felt comfortable telling her what was happening in their lives.

"When my son gets home from middle school every day, it's like a download," she said. "I ask, 'What books are you reading?'" Her kids tell her about their homework, their friends, the conversations they had on the bus. "Sometimes it's silly stuff," she said. Sometimes there's not much for her kids to report, and sometimes there is. Merianne says these conversations give her an opportunity to teach her children logic and help them discern between truth and nonsense.

## Listen to be a better advocate

Ohio mother-of-six Traci Woodard (winner of the 2024 Lori Cooney Lifetime Achievement Award) places a strong emphasis on communication—both talking and listening—as essential tools for raising self-sufficient, successful children. For Traci, maintaining open lines of communication serves a dual purpose: it helps shield children from negative influences and enables parents to become more effective advocates for their kids.

Normally, Traci opts to have her children excused from the school's sex education classes. However, one year, the family was out of town when permission slips were collected, and because of this timing, her daughter ended up participating in the class. She encountered information she wasn't quite prepared to process.

In response, Traci and her husband sat down with their daughter and engaged in a candid discussion about everything she had heard at school. Traci is a firm believer in creating a family environment where children feel comfortable asking questions without fear of judgment. A frequent phrase heard around the Woodard home is, "Mom, I have a question. Don't laugh." Traci encourages parents to approach these dialogues with realism and empathy, recognizing that children will inevitably encounter information that conflicts with their parents' beliefs.

Rather than avoiding or dismissing these conflicts, Traci sees them as opportunities. Through meaningful, respectful conversations, parents and children can navigate challenging topics together, fostering understanding and preparing children for future encounters with complex issues. "If your beliefs are different," Traci often tells her children, "Let's have a conversation about it." She encourages fellow parents to address issues proactively rather than letting them fester.

By listening intently to their children and nurturing these relationships, parents like Traci are cultivating an environment of mutual trust. This bond, once established, positions parents to be more effective advocates for their children, as they are closely attuned to their children's thoughts, feelings, and needs. In Traci's eyes, this connectedness isn't just beneficial—it's essential for families navigating the modern world.

## Be where your kids are

Whenever possible, be where your children are. If your kids attend a public or private school, consider volunteering in the classroom, chaperoning field trips, assisting at the school fair, or helping sell concessions at sporting events. This involvement allows you to build relationships with teachers and administrators and gain a firsthand understanding of the school environment.

By proactively engaging in this way, you are establishing goodwill with the individuals who play significant roles in your children's lives, positioning yourself as a trusted collaborator rather than a distant observer. Additionally, this involvement offers you the chance to familiarize yourself with your children's classmates and their parents.

However, it's important to set realistic expectations. Even committing an hour at the school each week, though valuable, won't entirely eliminate the potential for various issues that your children might encounter in today's educational environments. While your presence and involvement can be a powerful deterrent, it's not an absolute safeguard against exposure to challenges such as bullying, sexual harassment and abuse, access to drugs, and the relentless Marxist drumbeat.

If your goal is to protect your children from all these influences, more extensive measures may be necessary. This could include having open and regular conversations with your children about the issues they might face or exploring alternative educational options that align more closely with your ideals.

Remember, the key is to balance involvement with respect for your children's growing independence and need for autonomy. Engage, but also empower your children with the tools, knowledge, and confidence they need to navigate their own path responsibly and thoughtfully.

## Summary

- Know what's going on in your children's worlds.
- Listen to be a better advocate.
- Be where your kids are.

### Go Deeper

Watch Merianne Jensen's school board speech: https://twitter.com/DailySignal/status/1489669009490464772?s=20

## Chapter 7

# SEL Sounds Nice, But It's Not

Gabrielle Clark's life veered onto an unexpected path when her 12-year-old daughter began attending counseling sessions at her school in Las Vegas. Initially, Gabrielle attributed the changes she observed in her daughter's behavior to the lingering effects of lockdowns, but the picture grew more complex when her daughter befriended a classmate who identified as transgender.

Despite the evolving situation, Gabrielle remained hopeful. She desperately wanted to believe that the counseling was yielding benefits. She compared it to applying two coats of white paint over a black wall—a process she hoped was a necessary part of her daughter's healing. However, as time progressed, her daughter's personality underwent a profound transformation, leaving Gabrielle increasingly bewildered.

She started to understand what was going on with her daughter during a summer visit with a relative who lived in an area without internet access. Gabrielle's daughter reverted to her former, carefree self in just two weeks. However, as soon as they returned home, where her daughter regained internet access and contact with friends, the worrisome behaviors resurfaced. When school resumed and counseling sessions continued, things escalated dramatically: self-harm, destructive actions, and cruel remarks. Gabrielle would ask, "What's wrong?" only to be met with, "I can't tell you because you're not safe."

It was during this turbulent period that Gabrielle overheard a school administrator refer to her daughter by a boy's name. This was the moment she realized that her daughter's school was guiding her through a gender identity crisis, a journey that had shifted from identifying as bisexual, to lesbian, and then to non-binary. The school was no longer a safe place for her daughter. She would have to withdraw her and give her daughter a fresh start somewhere else.

Gabrielle pieced together the implications. Familiar with the SEL (Social and Emotional Learning) process, she realized that non-compliance with the counselor's approach could potentially result in Child Protective Services' involvement based on information collected through the program. She carefully began to devise an exit strategy. She wryly compared the process to fleeing a cult—a poignant irony for Gabrielle, an atheist.

Drawing upon her professional experience in domestic violence shelters, Gabrielle followed the same procedures to secure their escape. She severed ties with local friends, ensuring her daughter had no refuge to turn to if she chose to run away and return to Las Vegas. Gabrielle guarded her plans closely, entrusting the secret to just one person, her cousin, who generously offered an unfinished townhouse as a temporary home. It had plywood floors and no air conditioning, but it would give her daughter a safe, fresh start. Gabrielle even sold her car and parted ways with her fiancé, derailing their shared future. In other words, she threw herself over her daughter to protect her. Together, mother and her daughter packed their clothing, furniture, and cats into a U-Haul, and drove from Las Vegas to Houston.

Despite my assertion that Gabrielle is a hero, she humbly disagrees. "I don't know why any parent wouldn't do the same thing," she says, "especially if you know the result is your child mutilating themselves or becoming a trafficking victim. To me, I don't feel like a hero."

Today, Gabrielle Clark's daughter is a healthy, thriving high school junior. Gabrielle's sacrifices have paid off, and now she devotes her time to helping other parents whose children have been confused by online influencers, cultural winds, and their schools.

She continues to educate parents about the dangers of Social Emotional Learning (SEL). But where did SEL come from? And how did it infiltrate American schools?

## Paolo Freire's influence

Only a few years ago, SEL was largely unknown. Suddenly, it's everywhere. Where did it come from? And what do we need to know about it?

SEL was originally created to help students with unstable home environments. It sought to teach them ways to regulate their emotions and successfully interact in social situations. The goal was to make previously unmanageable students more manageable as they learned to better express and handle their emotions. Today, SEL is used in a blanket fashion, whether kids already have excellent social and emotional skills or not.

In its current form, social emotional learning uses a framework created by Brazilian Marxist educator Paolo Freire, in which children are taught what to think and how to believe. SEL "lesson plans" involve the Freirean concept of "conscientization," a process by which a child is made aware of the "truth" of reality. In our time, the "truth" that is being conscientized into our children's minds are the tenets of Marxist queer theory.

Linda Darling Hammond (from CASEL) is one of the architects of SEL. She wrote the forward to the 2015 book, "The Handbook of Social Emotional Learning in Research and Praxis." In her forward, she says that a school that's socially and emotionally competent is in line with Freire's project of transformation and humanization. Essentially, children will adopt Marxist consciousness. The idea is to use academic subjects as an excuse to have political conversations with children. SEL is the entry point to turn every academic subject into a social emotional subject, which is taught through a Marxist lens.

On the surface it may not seem that Marxism and the transgender movement have much in common, but advocates of Marxist ideology see the obliteration of traditional gender norms as necessary. In the book *Transgender Marxism*, Rosa Lee writes,

In a different era, Marxists spoke of the construction of a 'new socialist man' as a crucial task in the broader process of socialist construction.

Today, in a time of both rising fascism and an emergent socialist movement, our challenge is transsexualising our Marxism. We should think the project of transition to communism in our time...as including the transition to new communist selves, new ways of being and relating to one another.[24]

Traditional ways of "relating to one another" do not serve Marxists well. It's difficult to control young people when they feel loved and valued by their parents, siblings, and extended family. And it's difficult to control adults when their families are the center of their lives. Transgenderism, however, isolates people. Young people who are sterilized by sex-change surgeries don't have the same hope for fulfilling family lives in the future. In other words, transgenderism serves Marxist goals well.

But how can ideologues introduce Marxist queer theory to the rising generation? They need a nationwide education program. Why not use the federal Department of Education to help?

## ESSA, Common Core, and CASEL

People are often surprised to learn that the U.S. Department of Education has only been around since 1980. Before then, public education was completely governed at the local level. Since its establishment, taxpayers have poured money into the Department of Education, but all these additional funds and bureaucracy haven't boosted academic outcomes. Instead, K-12 education has been saddled with massive regulatory requirements, and schools must play by federal rules to secure funding.

The No Child Left Behind Act of 2001 was supposed to force schools to focus on struggling students, but it didn't lead to better outcomes. The Common Core State Standards Initiative followed in 2010. Forty-one states adopted the initiative, securing funding promised by President Barack Obama and Secretary of Education Arne Duncan. As we'll see in a later chapter, Common Core led to the abandonment of some traditional skills such as cursive handwriting. Then, in 2015, Every Student Succeeds Act (ESSA) was signed into law.

Schools must follow federal guidelines if they want federal dollars. Many people went along with No Child Left Behind (NCLB) because the principles behind it sounded promising. Everyone wants good schools, but how do you force them to improve? Without a solid strategy, administrators of the program started by measuring stuff. NCLB got schools accustomed to measuring and reporting data on each child: academic performance, truancy data, violence and drug-related offences, eligibility for special education, free and reduced lunch, country of birth, and language spoken at home. NCLB even collected students' home phone numbers and addresses and gave them to military recruiters.[25]

Next came Common Core. Parents and citizens focused on the strangeness of the Common Core curriculum (for good reasons). Suddenly, children were struggling with overly complicated math problems and teachers' insistence that they "deconstruct" texts in Language Arts. Common Core didn't come out of nowhere. It was a United Nations experiment, which was derived from the World Core curriculum. The bigger story about Common Core was that teachers' paperwork quadrupled. Suddenly, instead of spending time on lesson preparation, they were spending hours every day on paperwork to prove their Common Core teaching to the federal government so their schools could qualify for funding.

With the implementation of ESSA in 2015, schools had to start reporting on non-academic competencies. Let that register. In 2015, schools had to start giving non-academic data about students to the federal government.

Meanwhile, an organization called CASEL had prepared a ready-made solution for the non-academic competency reporting required by ESSA. CASEL (The Collaborative for Academic Social and Emotional Learning) was founded in 1994, and it lobbied to make sure ESSA got passed. The company was ready to send out their SEL program all over the country as soon as the federal bureaucracy required it. It worked like a charm. Today, 99% of school districts in the country are using CASEL's SEL products. The law created a requirement, and the product was ready to go at the moment it was needed. Now the schools are legally stuck with it, and CASEL is growing and growing.

ESSA outlined five core competency areas, which are perfect for constructing reporting requirements:

1. Self-awareness
2. Self-management

3. Responsible decision making
4. Relationship skills
5. Social awareness

At a time when half of students are not reaching reading proficiency, the federal government all but forced schools to focus on non-academic topics. Why?

## Implications of SEL

CASEL says that students with good social emotional skills perform better in school. But they don't have studies that prove that their program improves academic outcomes. They rely on people believing it—and it sounds good. We want to believe it. After all, our schools and students are struggling. Pew Research reports that "among the 35 members of the Organization for Economic Cooperation and Development, which sponsors the PISA initiative, the U.S. ranked 30th in math and 19th in science."[26]

So American K-12 academics are failing while the schools are creating vast stores of information about our children and teaching them to conform to Marxist values.

In 2020, CASEL announced an ideological shift to what they term "Transformative SEL." The concept, according to CASEL, is a "means to better articulate the potential of SEL to mitigate the educational, social, and economic inequities that derive from the interrelated legacies of racialized cultural oppression in the United States and globally." Longtime teacher Larry Sand put it this way: "SEL has become the therapeutic wing of the noxious Critical Race Theory. So now, kids are being radicalized and taught to feel good about it!"[27]

Not only does SEL take up valuable time that could be spent on reading, writing, history, mathematics, and science, but it also creates potential harms for American families.

At the beginning of this chapter, I told Gabrielle Clark's story about her daughter. She knew that the school had data about her daughter they could use with Child Protective Services. Other parents have reported that SEL surveys ask leading questions that cause children to mistrust their parents and put too much trust in other adults, as we saw with Gabrielle Clark and her daughter: "I can't tell you because you're not safe."

## Empowered parental engagement and advocacy

New York City teacher of the year (1989, 1990, and 1991) John Taylor Gatto said, "I've noticed a fascinating phenomenon in my thirty years of teaching: schools and schooling are increasingly irrelevant to the great enterprises of the planet. No one believes anymore that scientists are trained in science classes or politicians in civics classes or poets in English classes. The truth is that schools don't really teach anything except how to obey orders."

If you want your children to think for themselves, keep them far away from social emotional learning.

What can you do to combat the negative impact of SEL on your children? The most effective strategy is to avoid a school that spends time on SEL. If that's not an option, train your children to refuse to take surveys.

"Don't let them take the surveys," Merianne Jensen said, "and know that every minute spent on SEL is a minute that is not spent on reading, writing, math, science, and history."

Jensen teaches her children that schools are for learning academic subjects and that the school doesn't have a right to ask them personal questions. She calls SEL "critical race theory wrapped up in a different box." When it's time for SEL surveys, her children sit out in the hallway reading books.

"The younger we can start having our kids be different, the better off because an 8th grader, if they're not used to [being different], will feel insecure," she said. "So start young having them opt out of vision screenings, etc. It's not the school's job."

How young do schools start with SEL surveys? Kindergarten. They're collecting data from children who can't even read yet. "They have little smiley faces," Jensen said. "One of the questions last year was, 'How do you feel about masks?' They're starting young, desensitizing them so they can push their agenda down their throats. Their goal is to groom their kids for their agenda. It's really scary, and they know what they're doing."

Teachers are not therapists, and schools have no business collecting personal information about your children and family.

You must protect your children from ideologues who are actively recruiting disciples from our K-12 system.

## Summary

- The philosophical foundation for SEL hails from Paolo Freire's theories.
- The evolution of federal educational policy (ESSA, Common Core, and CASEL) helps us understand where SEL came from and how it secured widespread adoption so quickly.
- Implications of SEL.
- You can protect your children from the subtle messaging embedded in SEL.

### Go Deeper

*Transgender Marxism*. Pluto Press, 2021, https://www.plutobooks.com/9780745341668/transgender-marxism.

It's not a fun read, but this book leaves no ambiguity about the connection between Marxism and transgender activism. The publisher advertises it this way: "Reflecting on the relations between gender and labour, these essays reveal the structure of antagonisms faced by gender non-conforming people within society. Looking at the history of transgender movements, Marxist interventions into developmental theory, psychoanalysis and workplace ethnography, the authors conclude that for trans liberation, capitalism must be abolished."

## Chapter 8

# "When Anything Goes, Anything Can Happen"

In 1989, a miraculous, tiny baby girl was born to Rita and Guadalupe Velásquez in Austin, Texas. At just 2 pounds 10 ounces, baby Lizzie didn't give her parents or doctors much hope. Physicians told Rita and Lupe that their daughter would never walk, talk, or do anything by herself. In addition to her tiny size, Lizzie's body has no adipose tissue and can't create muscle, store energy, or gain weight. Even now, in her thirties, she has zero percent body fat and weighs just 60 pounds.

Despite these odds, Lizzie thrived, thanks to an optimistic outlook and amazingly supportive family. When she started kindergarten, she had no idea she looked different than everyone else. "It was a big slap of reality for a five-year-old," she said. But when she was 17, she found an 8-second video of herself on YouTube. It wasn't the content of the video that brought her to tears. It was the title: "The World's Ugliest Woman." Over 4 million people had seen the video when she first encountered it, and thousands of people had left comments.

Lizzie read every single comment, desperate to find even one person who would stand up for her. She didn't find one.

In a video later produced by *Allure*, Lizzie said that during this experience, she looked out her door. Her mother was watching TV directly in her line of vision. "I knew if that video crushed me as much as it did, I couldn't imagine what it would do to her." Lizzie knew she had steadfast champions in her parents. They were people who would have thrown themselves over her during a tornado. She knew that. And it gave her strength.

She realized that she could view her life any way she wanted to, and she chose to be grateful. "I can't see out of one eye," she said, "but I can see out of the other." She determined that the best way to get back at the people who bullied her was to improve her life and be happy. She wrote several books, graduated from college, and has had a successful career as a motivational speaker. I recommend showing your kids her TED Talk, "How do you define yourself?"[28]

## Bully education

Bullying is a problem in K-12 schools, and administrators often respond to the problem by establishing expensive anti-bullying programs. But studies have shown that these programs are not always successful. In fact, sometimes they make the problems worse.

Michigan State University conducted a study to explore the issue. They surveyed 7,000 students aged 12-18 and found that the students attending schools with anti-bullying programs reported experiencing bullying more than students who attended schools with no such programs. Some say students with anti-bullying programs are just more aware of the problem, and that's why they report it at higher rates. This could be. But other researchers allege that the programs actually help bullies to become better bullies. The programs give bullies new ideas and expose children to unnecessary roughness.

The attorney who defended me when I complained to the school district about the inappropriate assembly mentioned this phenomenon in his letter: "A primary concern of parents who hold to traditional views of the family, sexuality, and marriage is that so-called anti-bullying programs in the public schools are really just a cover for those who want to undermine traditional values. Your client's threat of a lawsuit gives credence to the concern that the true agency of the anti-bullying crusade is to silence those who dare to question the politically correct, but culturally harmful, embrace of gender confusion." In the assembly in question, which was presented to 11- and 12-year-old children, high school actors talked about homosexuality, hooking up, and more. How could such content improve the level of civility and decency in a school? It could not. Without a moral compass, district anti-bullying programs become conveyors of ideology and propaganda.

Clearly, leaving bullying prevention to the schools leaves your child vulnerable. There are so many tragic stories about what can happen when bullying runs rampant unchecked. I thought about including some of these stories here, but they're too heartbreaking.

Instead, I'd like to focus on what you can do to help your child respond to bullying like Lizzie Velasquez, and to minimize the chances of bullying in the first place.

## Bullying from peers

The number one way to minimize bullying from peers is to make sure your child spends his days in a moral environment. In 2017, GLSEN, an LGBTQ advocacy group, conducted a nationwide survey to learn about bullying. They subsequently produced "The 2017 National School Climate Survey" to publish their findings.

Unsurprisingly, district public schools turned out to be the most hostile place for LGBTQ students, according to the survey. Charter, private, and religious schools all proved to be more compassionate, moral environments. In these schools, GLSEN found fewer negative and biased remarks regarding gender, disability, immigration status, religion, body weight, and more.

Why is this?

For one, public schools have cast out religion completely. Most Americans still consider themselves to be members of a religion, and religion is where we get our moral codes. To create a space for children that eradicates religion is to usher in the *Lord of the Flies*.

Because they're public schools, charter schools leave religion outside the doors as well. So why do they have more moral environments (as GLSEN reports)? Parents often choose charter schools because of their focus on discipline. Many charter schools include some type of character education that focuses on personal responsibility, integrity, honesty, and other typical moral values, even if they don't explicitly talk about religion.

Private secular and religious schools scored best in the GLSEN study, and this is no surprise. When children spend their days in an environment where religious expression is welcome, everyone is kinder.

Additionally, the size of the school can make a big difference. Large district high schools have hundreds, if not thousands, of students to track. A smaller school is much more manageable in terms of bullying and the social scene.

Microschools have been springing up across the country, and this model can be an excellent option for children who have faced bullying in large district schools. With a group of just 10-12 students, bullying is much less likely, and the teacher has more influence on peer-to-peer social interactions.

Finally, homeschool can be an effective exit to a bullying situation. Time at home with loving parents can help a child heal from the wounds of bullying.

## Anxiety from 24/7 access to peers

But parents shouldn't be naïve about a bully's reach in today's culture. Gone are the days when kids only had to deal with negative peer interactions at school. With social media and smartphones, bullying can happen anytime, anywhere.

A 2022 Pew Research study found that nearly half of U.S. teens (46 percent) had experienced cyberbullying behaviors. While bullying has been a problem as long as people have inhabited Earth, previous generations have been able to escape it more successfully. At the end of a long school day, kids in the 1980s could go home and be pretty confident that they wouldn't hear from the bullies at least until school the next day.

With social media, however, today's students might find themselves scrolling through comments about themselves until the wee hours of the morning.

Consider limiting access to social media, especially during the hours when kids should be sleeping. And, as we talked about in Chapter 6, work on building a trusting relationship with your child. When your children know they can always talk with you about difficult interactions with peers, you can comfort and guide them.

## Identity formation

Adolescence is a key period for identity formation, and social media can hurt the process if it plays too large a role in a teen's life. For example, if young people start measuring their worth by how many likes their posts garner, they could start manipulating their personalities—just to get likes.

Instead of learning about themselves through hanging out with friends, finding out what kind of music they like, and taking up hobbies, many kids today—especially girls—try to develop their identities around what gets the most likes on social media. In many cases, popular posts are shocking in some way—revealing lots of skin, pulling stunts or pranks, or parroting popular or controversial statements. And once a post is on social media, it may always be around, even if it's deleted.

To help children develop their identities in healthier ways, parents can encourage kids to spend time with friends in person and put down the screens for extended periods each day.

Try working with your kids to establish certain screen-free times during the day, especially during mealtimes and for an hour or so before bed. The online world will always be there, and it will certainly still be around when it's time to pick up the phone again. In the meantime, kids can get to know themselves and the people they love through conversation, music, art, nature, athletics, and more.

## Sexual abuse

I wish I didn't have to write about this, but unfortunately, it's a cruel reality. During my school board campaign, a tragedy happened at Irving Middle School, my kids' school. A 22-year-old teacher named Jackson Hedrick was arrested on suspicion of first-degree sexual assault. The initial charge was enticement by electronic communication device (a class IV felony), but further investigation led to additional charges: private messaging, sexual contact, and furnishing the minor with alcohol.

While none of my children had had Jackson Hedrick as a teacher, he'd subbed for my 12-year-old's class, and she said everyone liked him. He was a youth leader at a local church that many of the students attended, and he helped coach the school's cross-country team.

How were these crimes uncovered? Did the girl's parents figure out what was going on? According to a local TV station,[29] "a social worker at a different school was notified by a student there of the inappropriate relationship and then police were informed."

Along with other Irving parents, I received an email from the principal, the very same principal who had shown such a lack of concern when it came to sexually inappropriate content in a school assembly. In the email, she told us that a teacher had been arrested "for enticement and first-degree sexual assault related to an alleged incident with an Irving student."

And then the letter got ironic. She continued, "Please take a moment to talk with your son or daughter about what to do if they or someone they know is uncomfortable in any way with an adult – either at or away from school. We encourage our students and families to report any concerning behavior that raises suspicion or concern – in students, staff or community members – to a caring, trusted adult. Our procedure at LPS focuses on the goal of creating a safe environment for all our students at Irving and Lincoln Public Schools."

When it came to a sexually inappropriate assembly, my daughter had done just that. She told a caring, trusted adult about the concerning behavior, and when I contacted the principal, the principal tersely said, "I'm sorry your daughter was uncomfortable at the assembly. Thank you for your feedback."

I didn't trust her, and I worried that other children were still at risk. As a part of my school board campaign, I had a blog, and I wrote a post requesting an investigation into Irving Middle School's hiring practices. This teacher had just been hired.

In fact, during Hedrick's sentencing,[30] the judge said the teacher started texting the 14-year-old girl *on the first day of school*, and 4,500 texts went back and forth between them.

The local paper, the *Lincoln Journal Star,* wrote an article about my blog post, and they interviewed one of my opponents in the school board race, Connie Duncan, who ended up winning the race.

In the *Journal Star* article,[31] Connie referred to Hedrick's crime as "a horrible mistake" and said, "shocking news is not to be totally unexpected." The article ended with another statement from Connie: "Contrary to what my opponent believes, ignorance never helped anyone make a better decision, nor protected a child from harm."

Protecting children from harm was one of my main goals for running for school board. I wish I could have been more ignorant of what was going on, but it was all too real and all too close.

A local talk show host, Coby Mach, had me on the show to discuss the crime, and he opened the show with this phrase, which has stuck with me all these years: "When anything goes, anything can happen."

And why not? When teachers are given license to talk about sex with students in the classroom, it's not much of a leap to talk about sex over text. By opening up the topic on the stage during an assembly, the grooming had begun. The students knew that sex and all the slang words to describe it were perfectly acceptable at school. Their teachers were cool with it, and they, the students, should be, too. And if they didn't feel comfortable with it, well, it was their problem.

I wish I could say that an event like this happens only once, that it was an anomaly that took place in a medium-sized town in Nebraska, and the rest of the country doesn't have to worry about it.

But sexual abuse happens in schools all the time.

Way back in 2004, the U.S. Department of Education published a comprehensive report about sexual abuse in public schools.[32] Their figures, based on a study from 2000 conducted by the American Association of University Women, found that nearly 10 percent of K-12 students in public school had been victims of sexual misconduct by public school employees. Based on those numbers, approximately 4.5 million children were suffering sexual misconduct at the hands of public school employees, with 3 million suffering sexual abuse. Incidentally, this number is 100 times greater than the physical abuse committed by Catholic priests, who were undergoing a serious public reckoning when the U.S. Department of Education published its report on sexual abuse at public schools.

Around this time, in 2005, Florida middle-school teacher Deb Lafave[33] pled guilty to having sex with a 14-year-old boy and didn't have to go to jail at all. She paid her debt to society through community service and probation.

In another, all-too-similar story, elementary school teacher Tennille Whitaker sexually abused four teenage students who were assigned to help in her classroom. When one of the boys rejected her advances, she would "get enraged, kick him out of her classroom and threaten to mark him absent," according to court papers.[34]

Court documents also revealed that the school district knew about Whitaker's behavior but failed to protect students. In one instance, a school worker walked in on Whitaker sitting on a student's lap, and later, a custodian caught the teacher alone with a student in her room with the lights off and the door locked.

Another teacher reported to the principal that she was in possession of a Snapchat photo of Whitaker having sexual relations with a student.

Whitaker set up her classroom to accommodate her liaisons with teenage victims. She created a "private reading area" that was not visible from the hallway or any windows.

Despite all of this evidence, the abuse continued, and in 2019, one of Whitaker's victims, 18-year-old Corbin Madison, took his own life because of the "resultant depression, humiliation and embarrassment."

Corbin's devastated parents sued Elko County School District (Nevada) for "failure to address, prevent and/or remove known sexual predators from its ranks." The lawsuit also stated that education officials "intentionally ignored multiple complaints regarding Whitaker that allowed Whitaker to sexually harass, molest and abuse children for several years."

Eventually, the school district settled out of court with the parents of the four victims in a $2.5 million agreement. Court documents claim that Principal Chris McAnany was warned six times that Whitaker was having "unlawful sexual relations with minor student." What was the response from the district's superintendent, Todd Pehrson? He issued a vacuous response eerily similar to the one emailed by my daughter's principal after Jackson Hedrick's arrest. Said Pehrson: "We follow our policies and procedures. The safety of our students is our number one concern at all times."

The safety of our students is our number one concern.

Obviously not. But what can you do as a parent or guardian to protect your children from predators when they're not with you. And keep in mind the sad fact that school isn't the only place sexual abuse takes place. Little League practice, Cub Scouts, and even church can be settings where predators take advantage of young victims.

Fortunately, there are many things you can do to reduce your child's chances of being victimized and help them know how to respond to dangerous situations.

Owen Lafave, the ex-husband of Florida teacher Deb Lafave, offered the following advice for parents on a podcast episode of *Crime Stories with Nancy Grace*.[35]

### *Use a tracking app*

Owen Lafave said that tracking apps wouldn't have helped his ex-wife's victim because such technology didn't exist back in the early 2000s, but today, it's easy to know where your child is always.

Sexual predators must get their victims away from witnesses, so they often take them to remote locations. Deb Lafave drove her 14-year-old victim 100 miles while his parents thought he was busy with extracurricular activities after school one day. An app like Life360 can help you keep tabs on your child and alert you to any abnormalities.

### *Drop in unannounced*

Mr. Lafave also recommends dropping in unannounced at your child's school or other activities. You can use any excuse you want or none at all ("Katie forgot her sweatshirt this morning" or "I just had some extra time during my lunch break"). By stopping in randomly, you can get a feel for what happens on a normal day, and you can keep other adults on their toes.

You might be surprised at what you find. While my kids were growing up, I built systems into my schedule that allowed me to pop in. For example, I volunteered to read to my 3$^{rd}$-grader's class on Thursdays after lunch recess.

One day, I arrived and found his classroom locked. I could hear children inside, so I tried to open it again. Nothing. I then knocked on the door, repeatedly and loudly, until one of the students finally heard my knocking and opened it.

The classroom was in chaos. Although the teacher was sitting at her desk, the room was in an uproar. Some kids had their shoes off, others were playing tag, and the whole room was a wreck. I quickly realized why nobody had heard my knocking: it was far too loud. But why was the door locked?

The teacher was not in there abusing students. She was sitting at her desk, jotting down notes in her grade book. Occasionally, she'd yell across the room to a student, "Olivia! What did you get on your paper?"

I couldn't believe my child was spending his days in this chaos. When the teacher finally noticed I was there, she told the kids it was reading time, and they gathered around me as I sat and read to them.

But when I left the classroom and walked down the quiet hallway, I felt restless and guilty. I couldn't leave my child in that situation. And I wouldn't even have known what was going on if I hadn't dropped by in the middle of the day.

### *Establish boundaries*

In the past couple of generations, the boundaries separating adults and children have blurred substantially. When I was a child in the 1980s, schoolteachers dressed professionally, and students dressed like children. Students were expected to always address teachers as Mr. Thompson or Ms. Hernandez, and there would have been no way for a teacher to communicate with a child who was at home.

But a relaxing in social norms and the advent of mobile communications technologies has made it possible for teachers like Jackson Hedrick to text students at any time of day or night. This is why it's essential that you teach your children to establish firm boundaries with adults, and the adults in your children's lives should understand your rules.

For one, teachers and coaches should not text students directly. If an adult needs to communicate with a child, the child's parent should be included in the text message or other method of communication. If this has been a problem in your family, don't allow teachers or coaches to have your child's phone number. They can send all the messages to you, and you can relay them.

If your children's school relies on email for student-teacher communication, check in on the email account every now and then, just to make sure everything is professional and aboveboard. This tip alone can significantly reduce the risk that your child will be a victim of a predator.

Besides communication, you can help your children establish boundaries by telling them they should never get into a teacher's car or spend time alone with them. And if they ever feel uncomfortable, they need to tell you or another trusted adult right away.

You don't want to instill a sense of skepticism or fear in your children, so many of these things can be communicated simply in the way you talk about them: "That's nice of Mrs. Williams to offer to drive students to the game, but it's not really appropriate for students to ride in coaches' cars. So I'm going to pick you up at school and take you. Feel free to see if any of your friends want to ride with us."

Teach your children to call adults by their last names. Your next-door neighbor is Mrs. Miller, not Kelly. If all the other kids on the street use first names for adults, this may feel awkward at first, but in my experience, other families find it refreshing and start adopting the custom as well. The words we use set the tone for our relationships, and some formal distance (and respect) between children and adults is healthy and more comfortable for everyone. We'll talk about this more in Chapter 14.

### *Set appropriate topics for child-adult relationships*

As my friend Coby Mach said, when anything goes, anything can happen, and that's why it's so important to set appropriate topics for child-adult relationships. If a stranger walked up to your child in a park and started talking about sex, you'd call the police. But if a guest speaker from Planned Parenthood shows up at your child's classroom and starts talking about sex, we're supposed to all act like this is acceptable.

It's not. Parents are responsible for teaching children about matters pertaining to their bodies and reproduction, and there are important reasons this should not be delegated to other people.

For one, parents know when their children are ready for these discussions. If they're addressed too soon or handled in an uncomfortable setting, kids will get embarrassed and may feel shame. And feeling shameful about your body or about the incredible gift of reproduction is a tragic beginning to the start of a family.

Also, values are an integral part of these discussions, and that's why public schools try so hard to insert themselves in the middle. They want to shape children's perceptions and values. But as we all know, sex education curriculum has an atheistic, hedonistic bent, which is at odds with many people's world views. Bottom line: it's risky to delegate your child's sexual discussions to other adults, and it sets up conditions that could compromise your child's notions about proper boundaries.

## Summary

- Be proactive to prevent and address bullying.
- 24/7 social media leads to anxiety.
- Consider how your children's experiences contribute to their identity formation.
- Protect children from sexual abuse.

### Go Deeper

Watch Lizzie Velasquez's TEDxAustinWomen talk about how we define ourselves. This is an excellent talk for young people to watch, especially at vulnerable times in their lives (like right before the first day of middle school). You can find it here: https://youtu.be/QzPbY9ufnQY.

# Part II - Prepare

## Chapter 9

# An Undereducated Public

You've likely come across those videos—the ones where an interviewer approaches people in a mall, on a bustling city street, or on a college campus and asks basic questions: Who fought in the Civil War? Name three continents. Who is the Vice President of the United States? The respondents often stutter and laugh nervously. When pressed, they offer an answer—frequently incorrect. The interviewer might nod approvingly, regardless of the response's accuracy, for the sake of engaging content destined to attract numerous clicks.

One hopes that these videos are selectively edited to show only the most bewildering answers. Perhaps these respondents are even acting, pretending ignorance for the sake of the clip. That is the hope. Yet, observing what teachers' unions and districts focus on, it becomes clear that these videos likely contain a kernel of truth.

You may have felt, as I have, that your own K-12 education was lacking in some vital way. In 2010, seeking more for my children, I enrolled them in the Colorado Online Virtual Academy (COVA), disillusioned by the offerings of our local school. I was immediately impressed with COVA's curriculum—engaging, well-constructed, and enjoyable. As I assisted my children with their schoolwork, I found myself learning, too. Particularly in history, I was encountering insights and facts as though for the first time. Remarkably, these bits of knowledge, drawn from books, documentaries, and my own scattered education, began to coalesce like pieces of a jigsaw puzzle snapping into place.

How, I wondered, with a bachelor's degree in hand, could I be learning so much from material designed for third graders? American education appears to have been on a downward trajectory for decades, suggesting that multiple generations of citizens have entered the adult world with less-than-ideal educational foundations.

How can parents ensure their children's education meets high standards when the very definition of "quality education" remains unclear? Before proposing solutions, we must first understand the magnitude of this challenge.

## K-12 in the United States

One way to compare how the United States stacks up against the rest of the world is to look at PISA results. PISA (Programme for International Student Assessment) is a test produced by the Organization for Economic Cooperation and Development (OECD), and it has been tracking student achievement around the world since 2000. Of the 79 countries tested, the United States comes in at about average in science and reading but below average in math. Andreas Schleicher, director of education and skills at the Organization for Economic Cooperation and Development, said, "About a fifth of American 15-year-olds scored so low on the PISA test that it appeared they had not mastered reading skills expected of a 10-year-old."[36]

And we can't feel better by looking at our own U.S. testing. The Nation's Report Card shows that only 28 percent of 4th graders, 26.4 percent of 8th graders, and 22.8 percent of 12th graders reach basic proficiency levels averaged across seven subjects (civics, geography, mathematics, reading, science, history and writing.[37] Take that in. Fewer than one in four high school seniors reaches basic proficiency levels. But that doesn't stop their schools from washing their hands of them after parading them across the stage at graduation. Many American public schools are failing their students, and we let them get away with it.

Since Covid, many parents have re-evaluated their roles regarding their children's education. After all, the teachers' unions coerced districts into closing schools and going remote, so parents finally got a peek into what their children were learning—and they weren't impressed.

Many parents were surprised to learn that the "experts" teaching their children seemed less educated than they expected. It's not necessarily the teachers' faults. Grade inflation is rampant in education departments at U.S. universities, and coursework is notoriously easy. Furthermore, students who major in education have some of the lowest ACT scores of all the students admitted to universities and colleges.[38]

One elementary education undergraduate I spoke with at the University of Nebraska - Lincoln said, "I've had eight or nine classes where the primary topic was racism. But what I really need is more instruction on how to teach math."

I asked her how many courses she'd taken that were helpful with math. "One," she said, "but we spent most of the time talking about Mayan number theory. And that's not what we use now."

So, if it seems that your child's teacher doesn't seem to know more about the topics at hand than you do, you're probably right. And yet, homeschool parents are often criticized for not being "certified."

What does it mean for our country when only a small percentage of the citizens have reached basic proficiency levels before leaving K-12? And why do so many people seem untroubled by this fact?

Like so many other topics in this book, much of the reason for the American educational decay can be traced back to dusty old Marxism. Do people in power want a populous with admirable skills in critical thinking, rhetoric, science, math, and history? Certainly not. It's difficult to control people who can see through gaslighting and propaganda. To have better control, it's best to give young people just enough education to work full-time, earn enough to pay taxes, and be prolific consumers.

But we parents cannot be satisfied with the standards of those who would like to control us and our children. Undereducated people have a harder time in life, specifically in these ways:

- **They may struggle financially**
- **They may make poor decisions**
- **They're susceptible to activist educators**
- **They lack resources to help others in times of need**

## Ill-prepared people suffer financially

Authoritarians don't want people to be financially self-sufficient. It's difficult to get people to want to rely on the government if they're happy to take care of themselves.

Today's power-hungry politicians keep trying to get people accustomed to relying on the government for money and services. Covid serves as a recent example of this. The government forced people to stay home from their jobs and sent checks to businesses and individuals, expanding eligibility for SNAP benefits, and extending unemployment benefits. As a parent, you know how this works. If your child knows you'll deliver his lunch to school every time he forgets it, he has no incentive to learn to be responsible. And once you've established the pattern, it's hard to break. If you deliver the lunch five times, he'll feel deprived and unloved when you say "no" on the sixth time. You've taught him to be entitled, and you've made him dependent on you. Power-hungry politicians understand this pattern. They want us all to depend on them for our lunches. But when we do, we lose our freedom, motivation, and dignity.

To maintain our self-respect and free agency, we need to be financially self-sufficient, and this is much easier to do with a solid education. People with excellent fundamental skills and knowledge can learn just about anything and are valued everywhere they go. When you make sure your children get a good education, you provide a solid foundation for the rest of their lives, and for the lives of your grandchildren as well.

## Undereducated people struggle to make informed decisions

During the years Poland fell under a communist regime, the authorities were constantly battling discontent among the masses. To keep people in line, the communist authorities replaced qualified, educated managers in the country's workplaces with unqualified, undereducated (but ideologically sound) personnel. These undereducated people enjoyed their new positions of authority, especially because they were tasked with acting as informants to the government on the activities of their co-workers.

By 1950, over 40,000 of these communist-sympathizing new managers were hard at work—not making sure their workplaces were running smoothly but writing and submitting reports. They produced hundreds of thousands of secret reports on their fellow workers, accusing them of corruption, anti-government attitudes, and many other crimes.[39] Between 1950 and 1952, 10,500 workers were arrested based on these reports, and, amazingly, some charges resulted in the death penalty.

Given the ideological bent infused in today's K-12 public education, it's not hard to see how this could happen, shocking as it is. How can you make sure your kids get the kind of education that will help them see through such sinister political machinations? Here's what they need.

### *Civic knowledge*

A quality education provides children with a broad understanding of the political system, democratic values, and rights and responsibilities of citizens. To be responsible citizens, children need to learn about their country's history, government structure, and the principles on which it was founded.

### *Critical thinking and analytical skills*

Education promotes critical thinking, analytical skills, and the ability to evaluate different perspectives. This empowers children to think critically about social issues, question prevailing narratives, and consider multiple viewpoints. They learn to analyze complex problems, assess evidence, and engage in constructive debates. These skills are crucial for understanding societal challenges and developing informed opinions on issues affecting their communities.

### *Ethical and moral development*

A good education nurtures ethical and moral development in children. It provides opportunities for discussions on moral dilemmas, ethical principles, and the importance of personal integrity. A well-educated child should have a finely tuned sense of right and wrong and be able to predict how policies and decisions will affect people and communities.

### *A healthy worldview*

Emotional people make rash decisions. But people with a well-rounded education are better able to see the big picture. Instead of relying on slogans and stories, they can critically think through policies and sort through candidates' voting records and promises. They've learned about the peoples and places of the past, and they can recognize patterns. They also have a firm foundation in mathematics and science, so they're not easily misled by illogical newspeak.

Well-educated people are less likely to fall for ridiculous political propaganda. Please keep in mind that when I say "well-educated," I'm not necessarily equating advanced degrees with education. Some of the best-educated people I know have never been to college--they're lifelong learners who have the intellectual humility to glean knowledge from many different sources. That said, when you provide your kids with a solid K-12 education, you not only help them to make informed political decisions, but you also strengthen the community at large.

## They're susceptible to activist educators

We had some friends who homeschooled their children for elementary and middle school but sent them to public school for grades 9-12. They were dismayed as, one after another, each of their five children fell away from their faith during their college years. How could this happen?

The kids' high school education had not prepared them to deal with the anti-faith and anti-western-civilization ideology that was relentlessly preached at the large state university their children attended. They didn't have the knowledge or tools necessary to think critically about their professors' arguments.

Lia Collings, a classically educated mother of eight, remembers facing this situation as an undergraduate herself and wants to prepare her own children to be ready to handle ideological conflict with logic. "I think pretty early on with my kids I wanted them to be an asset to the other students in their class," she said. "I wanted them to have read what the professors have read, so they don't have to just take what the professors say as the take on it, so they could say, 'Oh, well, yeah, you could say that, but couldn't you also say this?'" Lia believes when classical education was the norm, 18-year-old students were better prepared to talk with their professors because they'd already received formal training in literature and how to argue logically.

And professors are not the same as they used to be. Authors Joy Pullmann and Sumatra Maitra explain that "the rise of the activist professor in the academy has meant the emergence of a pattern in remaking a department's goals from a search for truth into an engine for socio-political change."[40] Truth is now treated as a naïve notion at most universities. The "capture" of the universities by the Marxist left has been a long time coming. Rudi Dutschke, a German socialist who was highly influential in the 1960s, suggested that a violent revolution in western societies was unlikely. Instead of an out-and-out revolution, [41] activists should instead bring about radical social change through "capturing" institutions and professions. The capture of universities is nearly complete.[42]

If you want your children to be able to withstand the persuasion of Marxist professors, you're going to have to teach them well. They'll need more than an anemic public-school education to ride out the four-year barrage of Marxist rhetoric.

But it's possible. And if, as Lia Collings suggests, your children can argue logically with their professors, they'll be a light to others. They'll strengthen their own abilities and show their fellow students how to resist. Intelligence and knowledge are not the same thing, and if your child is prepared with the necessary knowledge, they will be able to sift through university rhetoric and find truth on their own.

## They can't help others in times of need

In 1206, the Spanish priest Saint Dominic founded the Dominican Order, a Catholic order established to combat heresy through preaching, education, and intellectual pursuits. By the mid-sixteenth century, the order was established in Ireland, and the Dominican Sisters began founding convents and boarding schools in Dublin. They aimed to provide a basic education for poor Catholic girls to help them be productive members of society.

In the mid-nineteenth century, Father Thomas McNamara, who worked in a Catholic parish in Dublin, became aware of two young deaf girls, ages 8 and 9, who were in desperate need of education. He talked with Mother Columba Maher, the prioress of the Dominican Convent, about the girls, knowing the sisters' commitment to providing education for the less fortunate. Just days later, on January 11, 1846, the two deaf girls, Agnes Beedem (age 8) and Mary Ann Doherty (age 9) were admitted to the Dominican school. The problem was this: they'd never taught deaf students before, and none of the sisters knew sign language.

Father McNamara sent the two girls along with two Dominican nuns to France for six months to learn the teaching methods of Le Bon Saveur School. Having been trained in teaching and learning, these nuns, Sr Vincent Martin and Sr Magdalene O'Farrell, worked diligently to prepare to teach deaf students. On their return to Ireland, they opened St. Mary's Institute for Deaf and Dumb Females in September 1846 with 15 girls admitted to the program. It was hard going at first, adapting French Sign Language to English. But by the end of 1851, the program had grown to 100 pupils.

The sisters didn't stop there. By the mid 1860's, they had developed a vocational program for their students where the girls could learn basic training in cooking, laundry, dressmaking, sewing, knitting, and needlework. Not only were they opening the world to students who couldn't hear, but they were preparing them for a productive, satisfying, self-sufficient future.

Educating your children so they can take care of themselves is important. But why stop there? What we need are people who, like Sr Vincent Martin and Sr Magdalene O'Farrell, have the desire and capacity to help others in times of need.

Just think of the difference each educated person can make in the world. Unwilling to go along with damaging ideologies, these people have the skills and moral grounding to improve the lives of their fellow humans and resist the control of people who would use them for their own ends.

Setting higher academic standards for your kids might seem intimidating, especially if you didn't attend a challenging school yourself. Might your kids resent you for pushing them harder than their friends are being pushed?

Earlier, I mentioned a young man, Walter Blanks, Jr., who had struggled in various schools until his parents enrolled him in a challenging private school. He was held back a year and forced to stay in from recess until he caught up.

I asked Walter how he planned to educate his own children. He said, "I would start with what my parents started with: academic rigor, values, and the expectations placed on students during school—not just during school but whenever you step foot in the building. That was the biggest thing for me—the excellence demanded of me. It was super, super hard, but I'm incredibly grateful for that."

Overcoming challenges and meeting high standards doesn't seem to hurt children. In fact, it inspires them. What has Walter done since high school? He earned a journalism degree from Mount Vernon Nazarene University and works as a national spokesperson for the American Federation for Children. He travels the country speaking about education and writes for many publications you've heard of. The child who struggled to learn at school became a man who has the education and drive to follow his dreams—all because his parents took the reins.

Educator David Hardy believes in the success of pushing kids to excel, too. He knew that the young men at his inner-city Boys' Latin school could achieve incredible things if they worked hard, even when they took on challenges that most kids never attempt, like learning Latin. "You're empowering them to go take on difficult things. Everybody talks about inner-city kids. They're never encouraged to take on difficult things. If somebody whines, they say, 'Oh, let's kind of make it easier.' No! Go back and do it again. They never do that with stuff like sports. If you have a guy come in and say, 'Man, basketball's tough,' nobody says, 'Okay, we'll bring the net down lower.' No, you've gotta get out there and play.'"

Why don't we push kids in academics as much as we push them in sports? Hardy says we need to have the same attitude: "Go out there and learn it. And what that means is you have to be okay with failure because failure is what happens on the way to success."

In the years Hardy ran Boys' Latin, the students took the National Latin exam. "By the time I left, the middle school was killing it. They'd have like 70 guys take the test and 65 of them get a medal." American kids have great potential, much more than what national test scores show. Increase your expectations and watch them achieve amazing things.

## Summary

- K-12 in the United States is not doing well.
- Educate your children to succeed financially.
- Educate your kids so they can help others in times of need.

### Go Deeper

In 1983, the National Commission on Excellence in Education published "A Nation at Risk." A fierce call to arms, the report state, "If an unfriendly foreign power had attempted to impose on America the mediocre educational performance that exists today, we might well have viewed it as an act of war." The educational slide, begun when America abandoned classical education, had reached critical mass. It's interesting to read the report and compare the tone, statistics, and urgency to the rhetoric surrounding K-12 education today. Find the report in its entirety here: https://edreform.com/wp-content/uploads/2013/02/A_Nation_At_Risk_1983.pdf

# Chapter 10

# Returning to the Tried and True

For over a century, K-12 education in the United States has operated much like an assembly line. Children enter the system at kindergarten and emerge at high school graduation, often regardless of whether they meet critical benchmarks along their educational journey. In this conveyor belt model, promotion to the next grade is typically tied more to a student's age than to their mastery of essential material.

Given the less-than-inspiring results produced by this approach, it's no surprise that a growing number of parents and educators are looking to the past for guidance.

Susan Wise Bauer and her mother Jessie Wise published the "Bible" on homeschool classical education in 1999. Here's how it begins:

*If you're fortunate, you live near an elementary school filled with excellent teachers who are dedicated to developing your child's skills in reading, writing, arithmetic, history, and science. These teachers have small classes—no more than ten students—and can give each student plenty of attention. The elementary school sits next to a middle school that is safe (no drugs, guns, or knives). This school also has small classes; the teachers train their students in logic, critical thinking, and advanced writing. Plenty of one-on-one instruction is offered, especially in writing. And in the distance (not too far away) is a high school that will take older students through world history, the classics of literature, the techniques of advanced writing, high-level mathematics and science, debate, art history, and music appreciation (not to mention vocational and technical training, résumé preparation, and job-hunting skills).*

*This book is for the rest of us.*[43]

When they wrote *The Well-Trained Mind*, Wise and Bauer had spent a combined forty years in education, Jessie as a public and private school teacher and administrator, and Susan as a graduate student and college instructor. I love this line from their introduction: "You don't have to reform your entire school system. All you have to do is teach your own child."

## How do Wise and Bauer define classical education?

> It is language-intensive—not image-focused. It demands that students use and understand words, not video images.
>
> It is history-intensive, providing students with a comprehensive view of human endeavor from the beginning until now.
>
> It trains the mind to analyze and draw conclusions.
>
> It demands self-discipline.
>
> It produces literate, curious, intelligent students who have a wide range of interests and the ability to follow up on them.

Jeremy Tate, president of *Classical Learning Test* (CLT), said on a *2 Cent Dad* podcast, "Education didn't change very much for a really, really long time...Basically, what we would call classical education was really in place from the ancient world through the early centuries of the church, really through the beginning of the twentieth century." He goes on to say that a good education was rooted in philosophy and the classical languages, studying logic and grammar and rhetoric. "Everything that was kind of the meat and potatoes of a really good education has been stripped away," he said.

Tate says the founding generation of the United States of America would not recognize what we do today as education. "We don't do languages or philosophy; we don't do morality or religion or ethics. And what we do in terms of developing skills is very, very unclear." [44]

But an education that teaches Latin and Greek, philosophy, grammar, and rhetoric seems out of reach for most Americans today. And even if they could access it, what good would it do their kids?

In 2013, Fr. James Thornton[45] wrote about three benefits of a classical education:

- The preservation of knowledge, culture, and traditions
- The tools that enable students to become their own teachers throughout their lifetimes
- A broad-based, cohesive education focused on mastery

Let's take a closer look at each of these benefits.

## The preservation of knowledge, culture, and traditions

The highest priority of a classical education is to transmit the knowledge, culture, and traditions that our forebears preserved and passed on to us. Thornton quotes the Swiss historian Jacob Burckhardt: "We see with the eyes of the Greeks and use their phrases when we speak. But without an understanding of history, ancient languages, and philosophy, children don't even know where to cast their gratitude, if they feel any gratitude at all."

Today's so-called progressive education has a laser focus on the flaws of the past (slavery) and largely ignores the forward march of progress (Code of Hammurabi, Magna Carta, Declaration Independence, and the Constitution—which led to the abolition of slavery, at least in the West).

Our Colonial ancestors could read the ancients in the original languages. Therefore, they could identify errors in judgment in those early experiments with self-governance and create structures to prevent tyranny and collapse. How can we create a strong government without knowing what led to the decline of previous experiments?

So much of our world makes more sense when we know about the past. English is richer with a working knowledge of Latin, and today's troubles seem less dire when we can put them in the context of world history.

Our traditions make sense when we understand the world that created them, and children develop a healthy respect for the people who influenced the world as we know it today.

## The tools that enable students to become their own teachers throughout their lifetimes

Even for those who pursue graduate degrees, formal education only lasts for a fraction of a human life, but a vast, inexhaustible world of learning is before each one of us, if we only know how to teach ourselves.

Thornton says, "...the student is equipped to discern between that which is wholesome—contributing therefore to the uplifting of the mind—and that which is corrupting or debilitating. In other words, the student will be able to think critically and independently."

The phrase "critical thinking" has been terribly abused in progressive education. Many teachers use it to mean simply "agreeing with the Leftist, statist agenda."

Learning classical languages takes diligence and concentration, but if students gain an understanding of any one of them, they feel empowered to learn just about anything. Classically educated students are confident students. They can pick up a text and sort through its logic. They don't have to be told what a text means, and hopefully, if someone does explain it to them, they'll know whether or not that person is telling the truth.

## A broad-based cohesive education focused on mastery

A classical education is inherently broad, enough so that it can be put to work in any context. Consider the remarkable achievements of our country's first generation. These classically educated people founded universities (Thomas Jefferson), invented bifocal lenses (Benjamin Franklin), and created a constitution that has been copied by most of the world's nations. Could they have accomplished these feats if they'd been educated in today's U.S. public schools? Hardly.

Today's obsession with specialization has produced people who are educated only in one field, leaving them open to being blind-sided on most topics. In his 1948 book, *Ideas Have Consequences*, the American philosopher and historian Richard M. Weaver wrote, "It should be plain from the foregoing that modern man is suffering from a severe fragmentation of his world picture. This fragmentation leads directly to an obsession with isolated parts."[46]

You can help your children avoid obsessions with "isolated parts." A classical education provides a comprehensive framework they can build on as they learn and grow. When they learn about a historical event, they'll be able to mentally place it in the right spot on their historical timeline. The world increasingly makes sense to them.

On the other hand, children educated in so-called progressive schools are at the mercy of their current teachers. There's no overall framework, and there's no guarantee that they will be taught a solid core curriculum. That's why so many students graduate without even a basic knowledge of their own nation's history, let alone how that nation fits in with the rest of the world.

## What components are necessary for a classical education?

Keep in mind that these components haven't always been integral to a classical education, which was designed and refined over millennia. Remember that the Greeks' methodology was refined by the Romans, and medieval thinkers further honed it when Christianity became the major religion in Europe.

Classical education typically consists of seven liberal arts divided into the *trivium* and the *quadrivium.*

### *Trivium*

In medieval universities, students studied three subjects first: Grammar, Rhetoric, and Logic. The Latin word "trivium" means "the three ways" or "the three roads." At medieval universities like Oxford, the trivium was the principal undergraduate course.

Grammar: the study of language and its structure.

Logic: the mechanics of thought and analysis
Rhetoric: the use of language to instruct and persuade

To the ancients, the trivium's focus was the pursuit of truth, beauty, and goodness.

We see remnants of this classical system today in some areas. In England, Canada, and Australia, "grammar schools" are an option for young children (elementary school-aged children), just as they would have been in Greek, Roman, and Medieval times. If you search online for "grammar schools in the United States," you find all kinds of interesting statements like, "Grammar school is simply an old-fashioned term for 'elementary school.'" This isn't the case. America's elementary schools make no pretense of teaching the classical education trivium. America's elementary schools are a product of the Industrial Revolution, which aimed to prepare students to work in factories.

## *Quadrivium*

With a mastery of Grammar, Rhetoric, and Logic, students were prepared to tackle the quadrivium: arithmetic, geometry, music, and astronomy. Ancient Greek educators separated practical arts, which prepared students for trade and craftsmanship, and the liberal arts, which were focused on intellectual and moral development. "Liber" comes from the Latin word meaning "free." Therefore, a liberal arts education aims to prepare students to be free thinkers, while vocational education aims to prepare people to be skilled workers in specialized trades.

According to Robert Littlejohn and Charles T. Evans, a liberal education produced "individuals who were skilled, lifelong, independent learners having no further need of tutelage and who, through their continued self-directed learning, would become wise and eloquent servants in their societies."[47]

Classical education spread from the Romans to Britain in the year 78, when the Roman governor Agricola decided that the Britons he ruled should adopt the Roman way of life. He provided a liberal education to the sons of local chieftains "so that those who had lately rejected the language of Rome now wished to acquire eloquence."[48]

The legacy the Romans left to Britan continued after Rome fell, and the Middle Ages saw the rise of universities. Knowledge of ancient Latin and Greek allowed medieval scholars to rediscover the scholastic philosophy of Aristotle, the medicine of Hippocrates, and the theology of the Greek New Testament.[49]

The pinnacle of medieval studies (available to students who mastered the quadrivium) was the pursuit of philosophy (which included science) and theology. If you've ever wondered why a person with a doctoral degree in Chemistry is a "Doctor of Philosophy," all you have to do is think medieval. Philosophy used to encompass science.

All of this is interesting, but what does it have to do with 21st century American children? And is it possible to find or construct a classical education for your own children?

We'll return to classical education toward the end of the next chapter, but first, we'll look at the various K-12 education options available in the United States today.

## Summary

- Classical education has three main benefits: the preservation of knowledge, culture, and traditions; the tools that enable students to become their own teachers throughout their lifetimes; and a broad-based, cohesive education focused on mastery.
- Classical education usually follows the Trivium model, focusing on grammar, logic, and rhetoric.

### Go Deeper

Bauer, Susan Wise, and Jessie Wise. *The Well-Trained Mind, 4th Edition*. Norton, 2016.

Even if you aren't planning on homeschooling your children, reading this book will change your perspective on education. You might even want to improve your own knowledge base because you'll realize your own K-12 education was spotty at best. It's a terrific reference book to have around your home, so purchase one if you can. Because it's been in print for so long, it's easy to find used copies. I really can't praise this book highly enough.

## Chapter 11

# Find the Best Educational Options

David P. Hardy is no stranger to K-12 education. He was the co-founder and CEO of Boys' Latin in Philadelphia, a single-sex charter school with a student body that is 98 percent African American and 74 percent economically disadvantaged. He's currently serving as the interim president of Girard College, a historic boarding school in North Philadelphia, which educates children from single-parent households.

So, when it came to educating his own two sons, Hardy had definite ideas. Initially, he enrolled them in a single-sex private school. "They liked it up until they got to be in middle school," he said. "Then they wanted to go to a co-ed school. But they got a strong foundation." Hardy asserts that single-sex education is most important in the early years. "If you set a second-grade boy next to a second-grade girl, the boy does not look like he belongs." He believes that boys will be more confident students if they begin their education in boys-only schools.

After mastering basic skills in elementary school, Hardy's sons' paths diverged. He noticed that his younger son was very quiet in high school. So "what we did is we enrolled him in what's known here as the Pennsylvania Leadership Cyberschool," he said. "They had a fine arts program where you do online school Monday, Wednesday, and Friday, and Tuesday and Thursday you go to Westchester, which is about 25 miles outside the city. They had music, dance, drama, all the arts, and he's an artist." Hardy didn't know that his son had artistic talent, but once his son was enrolled in an arts school, he "really got into it. And he was a better student."

Hardy had concerns about a cyber school, however. He wondered if he and his wife would end up having to nag him to get his work done. "But we never had to do that. He took ownership of his work, and he really liked the idea of going out there and being with all these artsy kids and everything two days a week. He did well there, and he went to the university and took up animation."

The bottom line for Hardy? "You have to find what each child needs."

Shouldn't children growing up in the same household receive the same kind of education? When Hardy and his wife found out they were going to have a second son, he said, "'Wow, this is going to be easy. I already have a son. Same house, same food, it's a rerun. They couldn't be farther apart. They're nothing alike!' And I should have known better. I'm a teacher! Wishful thinking is what it was. But the fact is once you have two kids you know that no two kids are alike. Three kids? Three different people. Ten kids? Ten different people. So the idea that you could have one school to serve all the kids in any one neighborhood or one city, that's crazy! "

Ohio mother Traci Woodard and her husband have six children: two graduated from private school, two from career tech schools, and two will graduate from virtual school. She said, "At some point, all of our kids have been virtual online learners, or some have been brick-and-mortar learners, but the big thing is to find out what makes them tick."

Traci's second son, Walter, struggled early on in his academic career. "It was all over the place," he said, "and I was in a different school almost every single year. My family tried community schools, charter schools, public schools, homeschooling, like everything, and I just couldn't find the right environment that was conducive to my learning needs. I was either too big of a distraction or my attention couldn't be maintained. I was just all over the place. I really struggled. I was also bullied a ton in the public school system. It just wasn't a very good place for me all around." We'll come back to Walter later on. But by now, you might be thinking, "I've got to make changes to my kids' educations." If that's what you're thinking, you're not alone. A 2022 poll by National School Choice Week found that 52% of parents had considered new schools for their children within the past year."

It's a different world than it was 30 or 50 years ago. The neighborhood school might be completely inadequate for teaching your children "good basic skills" like Hardy's sons received in elementary school. Also, what works well for one of your children might not work at all for another.

The good news is that school choice is growing across the country, and that means there are more schooling options than ever before. Additionally, education entrepreneurship is flourishing, which means that more and more options will be developing in the years to come.

Some states are further along in providing multiple education options for students, so you may not be able to find all the following models in your local area. If you find your options lacking, talk to your state legislator about expanding school choice opportunities.

Let's look at options that might be available in your area:

## District Public Schools

District public schools, also known as traditional public schools, are educational institutions that are funded and operated by local school districts or government entities. These schools are typically open to all students residing within a specific geographic area, and students are assigned to schools based on their residential address. As such, there are wide discrepancies in quality from neighborhood to neighborhood. District public schools have an incredible amount of funding, thanks to union and stakeholder lobbying. But ever-increasing funding has not led to improvements in outcomes.

Some parents stick with district public schools for the extracurricular activities, which are often well-funded and excellent. For example, a child who excels in football may want to attend a large public school for the opportunity to play on a large team. Keep in mind, however, that many states have laws that allow any young person to participate in public school athletics, even if they're homeschooled or attend a private school. After all, you pay for public school whether or not your children attend.

In the past few years, district public schools have become epicenters of cultural clashes. You've seen the videos of school board meetings. Parents use the public comment time to read passages from pornographic books stocked in school libraries or to object to policies about locker rooms and sports. If the parents don't like the school's policies, why don't they just withdraw their children?

It sounds reasonable until you think about education funding. In most states, a child's education funding automatically goes to the neighborhood district school. If the parents want to homeschool or enroll their child in a private school, they forfeit their child's funding and pay for the education themselves, even though they keep paying their taxes. If parents could direct their kids' funding wherever they wanted, these school-centered cultural clashes would dwindle and maybe even disappear.

The monopoly structure of the public schools leads to strange dynamics. Since the schools must accept every student—and often they're ill-prepared to teach some students—they claim to be under-resourced. David Hardy put it this way: "No matter how much money they have, they always need more money. So, they always come off as being underfunded--they're living on a shoe-string budget. The other thing is that all the kids have all these problems. 'They're lucky we can even teach them to walk with all these maladies, and we're finding new ones every five minutes. We're saints, stuck in here with these weird kids you keep sending us.'"

This description may not apply to your local public school, but many parents and teachers find the description all too familiar.

## Homeschool

With homeschooling, parents or guardians take on the responsibility of educating their children at home instead of sending them to traditional schools. This option provides the flexibility to tailor the curriculum and learning environment to the individual needs and interests of the child. Homeschooling allows for personalized instruction, one-on-one attention, and the ability to adapt to the children's pace of learning. Parents can incorporate various teaching methods and resources, including online materials, textbooks, and hands-on activities. This option also provides opportunities for experiential learning outside of the traditional classroom setting. Homeschool has been growing steadily over the last few decades, so it's easier all the time to find local community co-ops and activities for homeschooled children.

Michelle Kelso Kafer asserts that there's never been an easier time to homeschool, and I agree! "Homeschool is a style of life, and not everyone wants that style of life," she said.

As you choose learning methods and curricula, Kelso Kafer recommends writing down your goals and principles and asking the following questions:

- **What kind of lifestyle and structure do we want to achieve?**
- **What kind of extracurricular activities are important?**
- **What kind of teacher are you?**

"If you find that a curriculum isn't working, switch," she recommends. "Trial and error are okay." And don't feel like you must be an expert. You can learn with your children. Michelle is learning Latin along with her children, "and it's not as overwhelming as it sounds." She also advises parents to avoid falling into this trap: "If you're transitioning from public school to homeschool, don't feel like you have to model the structure of public school. It's a different environment. It takes time. Your first year of homeschool will be a lot of trial and error and learning how things work. There will be some awkwardness, and that's okay."

Some parents find that homeschool can be a great temporary solution to make it through a difficult year or overcome a specific challenge that school has failed to address. It's an option with maximum flexibility and the potential to bring families closer.

## Online schools

Online education has become increasingly popular as a flexible and accessible option for students of all ages. It allows students to learn remotely through digital platforms and virtual classrooms. Online education offers a wide range of courses and programs, from K-12 education to higher education and professional development.

Students can access educational materials, lectures, and assignments online, and often have the flexibility to learn at their own pace and schedule. Online education provides opportunities for self-directed learning, collaboration with peers through online discussions, and access to resources and expertise from around the world.

Two of Traci Woodard's sons attend an online charter school called Connections Academy. They learned to be responsible for their own learning, making appointments with their teachers when they needed extra help and budgeting their time as they worked through schedules.

Some online schools operate as charter schools. That means they're public and don't require any out-of-pocket cost to families. Others operate as private schools that collect tuition from students. Additionally, some may operate in your local area and provide field trips and other extracurricular activities. Or, you might find that an out-of-state or even out-of-country online school becomes accessible to you—this can be an incredible help for families living in rural locations.

## Charter schools

Charter schools are publicly funded schools that operate independently under a charter or contract with a governing authority. They have more freedom and autonomy compared to traditional public schools, allowing them to implement innovative educational approaches and curriculum. Most charter schools operate independently of teachers' unions, which is why you'll hear so many negative things about them. The unions really hate losing out on regular dues (and influence) when teachers transfer from district to charter schools.

These schools often focus on specific themes or educational philosophies, such as STEM (science, technology, engineering, and math), arts, or Montessori education. They are accountable for meeting specific academic goals and outcomes outlined in their charter. Charter schools can provide parents with additional educational options within the public school system.

Our family has had several experiences with charter schools, and the major difference we've noticed between district and charter schools is that the charters seem more focused on academics. For instance, at The Academy charter school in Westminster, Colorado, assemblies were focused on student achievement—especially giving awards to students who had worked hard and made big improvements. At our kids' district schools, assemblies often focused on social issues.

Charter schools often have waiting lists, so if you're considering enrolling your new kindergartener in one, start looking early. And don't be afraid to ask for tours. Spending time in a school is the best way to learn about the environment.

## Private schools

Private schools are independent educational institutions that are privately funded and not operated by the government. They often have their own unique mission, educational philosophy, and admissions criteria.

Private schools offer diverse educational approaches, such as religious-based education, Montessori, Waldorf, or college-preparatory programs. They typically have smaller class sizes, specialized facilities, and dedicated faculty. Private schools can provide a more tailored and rigorous education, with a focus on academic excellence, character development, and extracurricular activities.

Fortunately, private schools are more accessible than ever before, thanks to private school choice programs like vouchers, ESAs, and tax-credit scholarships. Also, private schools typically educate kids for far less than district public schools.

Some parents never consider private schools because they assume they're only for wealthy families. While it's true that some schools are so expensive that only the wealthy could afford them, you might be surprised by the affordability, especially if you live in a state that offers vouchers or ESAs.

People involved with the government school establishment also like to insinuate that private schools don't offer services for children with disabilities. But many parents have found that a private school has been able to help their children when public schools could not. It's worth exploring all of your options.

## Microschools

Microschools, also known as micro-learning communities or micro-education centers, are small, localized, and often unconventional educational settings designed to provide personalized and flexible learning experiences for students. These schools typically have a very small student population, usually just 8 to 12 students, and are often led by educators, parents, or community members.

The innovation of microschools is happening mostly in states that have passed ESA (Education Savings Account) legislation. ESAs give parents the ability to direct all or a portion of their children's education funding to schools or education resources that best meet their needs. Arizona was an early pioneer of ESAs, and as such, the state is seeing burgeoning innovation in the K-12 sector.

For instance, the organization Prenda was founded in 2018 by Kelly Smith, a former Google engineer and entrepreneur. The organization's inception was inspired by Smith's desire to reimagine education and create a more effective and personalized learning experience for students.

Since parents can direct their kids' funding, they can pool it to hire a teacher to educate a small group of children. Prenda has developed systems and curriculum to make it easy for parents and teachers to organize and run microschools.

As you can imagine, a school of 8-12 children offers personalized instruction, flexible schedules, experiential education, and an emphasis on relationships and the broader community.

## Hybrid approach

Hybrid education combines elements of different educational approaches, such as in-person instruction and online learning. It blends traditional classroom instruction with digital tools and resources. Hybrid models vary widely and can be customized to meet the specific needs and preferences of students and families.

Some hybrid programs may have students attending school in-person for part of the week and completing online coursework for the remainder. Others may integrate online components into classroom instruction, allowing for personalized learning and additional resources. Hybrid education offers a balance between face-to-face interaction and the flexibility and individualization of online learning.

When parents can't find exactly what they're looking for, they sometimes create a hybrid model of their own. We did this for several years when our kids were in high school. We homeschooled for several core subjects, like English and math, used the district schools for choir and athletics, and supplemented with online classes and community co-ops.

## Classical education

Classical education isn't a model like the other categories mentioned above. It's more of a philosophy or approach to education.

If you're seeking a classical education for your children today, you're not likely to find it in district public schools. But more and more, parents can find classical education instruction and resources in private schools, charter schools, microschools, and homeschool co-ops, or they can create it at home.

Utah mother Lia Collings has sent her children to different kinds of schools (public district, homeschool, and charter), but she has always aimed for a classical education. "Classical education has worked for centuries. That's why it is so amazing," she said.

Collings wanted her children to develop confidence in their ability to learn, so she taught them Latin. "Latin is super, super demanding," she said, "and if you can do that, you can do everything. Latin is like a 2-mile morning run for your brain." For a time, she took care of Latin instruction at home, and then she found a classical charter school that continued her kids' ancient language education.

Tennessee mother Michelle Kelso Kafer is learning Latin alongside her children. "We laugh a lot," she said. "If we mispronounce it and totally botch the word, then we listen to the pronunciation and just laugh because it's fun." Kelso Kafer insists that learning Latin with your children is not as overwhelming as it sounds, and she agrees with Collings on the benefits. Michelle says her kids pick up on words that she would never expect them to understand when they're studying science or history or geography or medicine. They recognize the root words from Latin. "It's almost like a hidden treasure for them: they actually understand what bioluminescence is, just from seeing the word."

At a time when American K-12 seems to be crashing and burning, returning to a type of education that "has worked for centuries" seems like a good idea. And the trend is growing. Beginning in the early 2000s, some private schools—and even a few charter schools—started advertising classical education. It took a few years to gain traction. The Virginia-based Veritas School was founded in 1998, and its original cohort had only 25 students. By 2009, the school had outgrown its original space, and by 2022, Veritas School had over 600 students enrolled in every grade from kindergarten through 12th.[50]

## "Fixing" the public schools

As I speak with parents in various areas, I'm often asked, "Why don't you try to fix the public schools?"

It's a valid question, and I don't fault anyone for trying. But here's the thing. I tried. I tried and tried and tried. And in the meantime, my kids were growing up before my eyes.

I wrote strongly worded emails to the school (and we saw how that turned out). I attended many school board meetings and used my allotted five minutes to speak to people who stared at me with glazed-over eyes. I wrote letters to the editor and blog posts about my concerns. I even ran for school board, walking door to door in my community to talk with other residents about the issues facing our children. Nothing noticeably changed. So finally, I started a school choice organization and testified repeatedly at the state legislature about bringing more options to our communities.

It was a lot of work, and in 2023, Nebraska finally passed one piece of school choice legislation—two and a half years after my youngest child left for college. Did all of my efforts fix the public schools? No. I hope my efforts helped future kids, but in the meantime, my own children needed a decent education.

The chart below illustrates the situation.

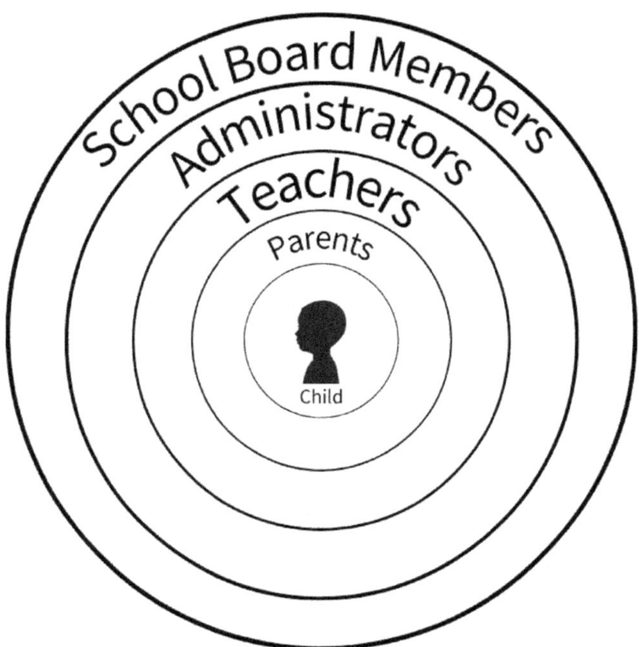


**Spheres of Influence**

The child is in the center, and the people closest to the child are his parents. They've known the child his entire life, and they see his day-to-day moods, interest, challenges, and triumphs. Obviously, parents are in the best position to make decisions for the child.

If the child is enrolled in school, his teachers have the next most influence on him. They see him most days of the week for a good chunk of the day. However, teachers typically only see the child at a certain age. They didn't know him as a younger person, and they have no expectation of having influence in the future.

Next, school administrators have some influence over the child. They set policies about the schools he attends, and they control some of the funding. Chances are very good, however, that they don't even know the child's name.

Finally, we have the school board members. They're politicians who might serve in that role from a few years to several decades. Not only do they not know the child, but they may have not even been to his school before.

So why, when parents have a problem with their children's educations, do we go to the school board? They don't know our kids. They don't have much invested in our kids.

We talk to them because they hold the purse strings for our kids' educations. And if you live in an area with little or no school choice, you may have very few options. Aim to rely on those inner levels of the circle as much as possible. Children get the best results when the people closest to them make decisions. After all, those are the people who know them best.

That said, many parents have made a difference in their schools and communities by voicing their opinions to the politicians who hold the purse strings.

Merianne Jensen is one of those parents. And she might be familiar to you. After all, the speech she delivered to the Prince William County School Board in February of 2022 went viral. Within days, nearly a million people had listened to her remarks about masks in schools. Her courage was infectious, and she gave other parents and students a model of how to stand up for their rights.

"I felt very strongly that I needed to speak at a board meeting because I had so much anger," she said. "I had emailed, I had done everything I could, short of showing up on their doorstep.

They were not listening. I thought, the only way I'm going to be able to express myself is to get to a board meeting. And I had been to several board meetings before, and I was never able to get a spot. They were really strict, very in control about how many people can speak. We can't hold up signs, we can't cheer. So, I think it was all God's timing that I got a spot to speak. Honestly, I really feel like that. And I got up and I gave my speech, and I didn't think anything of it and came home, went to bed, woke up the next morning and had Laura Ingraham calling me, Newsmax, and Clay Travis and all that. After that, I still felt like there were things I needed to do."

One school board speech, even an impassioned speech that inspires others, will not fix all the problems you face with your children's schools. If your kids' school meets their needs and maintains a wholesome environment, you can probably fine-tune the problems. If, on the other hand, the problems are overwhelming, put your children first and find alternatives. There's too much at stake.

## Seeing K-12 as a menu of options

When you start to look at K-12 education as a menu of options, it's exciting. You don't have to just tolerate whatever it is that local school administrators think is best for your children. You're in the driver's seat.

You can look at each of your children and ask questions like these:

- What kind of environment will help this child fulfill her potential?
- What school works best for his learning style and interests?

- Which schools most closely reflect our values and philosophy?
- Which school will help us maintain our preferred lifestyle?
- Which schools respect my parental authority?
- What kind of curriculum will best prepare my child for the future?

You don't hear these kinds of questions from district public school teachers and administrators because they're one-size-fits-all. They can't be bothered about individual children's values, dreams, traditions, and goals. But by taking control of your children's educations, you can give your kids the best foundation for the future.

## Summary

- Explore the various types of K-12 education models: public, private, homeschool, charter school, online school, micro schools, classical education.
- Start seeing K-12 as a menu of options. You may be able to craft a custom schedule for your kids that includes various resources.

### Go Deeper

Campanella, Andrew. *The School Choice Roadmap: 7 Steps to Finding the Right School for Your Child*. Beaufort Books, 2020.

Andrew Campanella is a school choice expert and a lovely person. He wrote *The School Choice Roadmap* to help parents navigate their options. It breaks down the similarities and differences between traditional public schools, public charter schools, public magnet schools, online public schools, private schools, and homeschooling. *The School Choice Roadmap* also provides a process to help you discover which of your options might be the most appropriate for your children: good, practical advice.

# Chapter 12

# What to Look For in a School

If you haven't ever thought outside the parameters of your local neighborhood public school, the process can seem overwhelming. What should you look for? How will you know which option is best for your child? Where should you start? What if you choose poorly?

Fortunately, you're not committed to sticking with your initial choice. If you find that the school isn't a good fit, you can always change it later. And although it's not ideal to move your child around much, it's better than keeping her in a bad situation.

Your priorities may differ from your neighbor's or sister's, and that's fine. If you haven't yet taken the time to reflect on what you want most from your child's education, consider the following exercise as a starting point. As you read through a list of educational attributes, notice which ones resonate most strongly with you. This self-awareness is the first step toward making informed and intentional decisions about your child's education.

In the following sections, we'll explore various aspects to consider when evaluating different educational options. Hopefully, you'll start envisioning how certain options align with your family's priorities and your child's unique strengths and needs. Knowing what you value is the key to finding an educational path that feels not only manageable but inspiring.

## Academic Quality

Some schools focus more on academics than others. You can assess a school's academic quality by reviewing its curriculum, teaching methods, and student performance data. If this is a high priority for you (and it's probably the most common priority for parents), learn how to read the signs that a school cares about academics.

### *High expectations*

Mediocrity is a pervasive issue in American education, making it a challenge to find schools that uphold high expectations for student achievement. A significant part of this problem stems from the quality of education provided to future teachers. A study by Cory Koedel at the University of Missouri revealed that education majors tend to enter college with the lowest average SAT scores yet graduate with the highest GPAs.[51]

Koedel speculates that the lenient academic standards in education departments at universities may set a precedent for low expectations that continues when these individuals become teachers in the K-12 school system. He points out a notable parallel between the generous grades awarded to prospective teachers during university training and the favorable evaluations these teachers often receive once they are working in schools.

Given this systemic issue, what steps can you, as a parent, take to find a school that insists on high academic standards?

### *Evidence of post-secondary success*

Educational consultant David Hardy advises parents to look for schools with a strong track record of post-secondary success. It's common for schools to boast high graduation rates as a selling point, but these rates can be misleading. For instance, a 90% graduation rate loses its luster if only 40% of those students achieve basic reading proficiency.

A more telling indicator is the success of students after they complete their K-12 education. For those attending a college prep school, consider how many are accepted into four-year universities, and how many of these students ultimately graduate from college.

### *A priority of academic success*

Schools committed to high academic standards often meticulously track and openly share these statistics. They invest in their students' success and remain invested in their journeys after graduation. Take, for example, the Denver School of Science and Technology (DSST) charter schools. DSST proudly shares that 100% of their graduates have been admitted to college since 2008. In the class of 2022 alone, DSST celebrated 5 Questbridge Scholars and 2 Daniels Fund Scholars, with an average of $2.5 million in scholarships and grants awarded per school.

What is particularly striking about these accomplishments is the socioeconomic background of the students DSST serves: 73% qualify for Free and Reduced Lunch. A personal anecdote further illustrates the culture at DSST: several years ago, my husband taught a robotics course at the original DSST high school in Denver. He was profoundly struck by the teachers' deep commitment to their students and the students' discipline and focus—an atmosphere that stood in stark contrast to another public school where he taught that semester.

In today's educational landscape, creating an environment that prioritizes student achievement over social engineering is nearly a counter-cultural act. But such schools do exist, and with diligence and focus, you can find them for your child.

### *Teaching Staff*

You probably have a favorite teacher in your past, someone who challenged and inspired you at a critical point in your development. Does your child's school have teachers like that? Do the teachers at your child's school have similar values to you?

In the last few years, we've seen many social media videos of teachers who use their positions to indoctrinate children with gender ideology and other Marxist philosophies. Can you trust the teachers at your child's school to stick to academics? Will they view your child as a sovereign individual with a bright future or as a potential convert to their worldview?

These are serious questions, and you, as a parent, have every right to know who your child will spend his days with. There are some real heroes out there, like the teacher who alerted me to gender ideology documents in my kids' school back in 2014. When you find teachers like these, build them up and thank them. They're swimming upstream, and it's exhausting.

### *School Culture and Values*

There's a myth out there that only private schools can "have values." All schools have values, just as all people have values. Your values are simply your priorities. What do you value most? What does your child's school value most?

Sending your child to a school that has values that conflict with your family's can have significant long-term consequences. Do you really have time in the evening to undo all the messaging your child receives between 8 am and 3 pm? Is it even possible to know what has been said during all those hours?

Sadly, many parents have recently realized that schools have no problem coming between children and parents. In fact, some teachers consider it their responsibility to "correct" the values and ideas that children learn from their parents.

This is why it's so important to find a school that has a culture and values that harmonize with your family's culture and values.

It's not hard to tell. Here are some clues:

- Posters/artwork: what kind of images will your child see at school every day? Are they political or ideological in nature? Are they academic? Are they inspiring?
- Assemblies: do administrators use precious assembly time to reinforce learning (awards for students who have achieved excellent academic outcomes or attendance benchmarks) or to introduce students to administrators' pet interests, like the alleged anti-bullying assembly that left my daughter in tears?
- Curricula: do the books and educational content used by the school reflect your values? Of course, children can and should be exposed to all kinds of ideas. But how are these ideas presented? For example, is your religion portrayed in a negative light by the school's curriculum? Is your home country maligned and treated disrespectfully by books your child is assigned to read?

## *Facilities and Resources*

District public schools often tout their luxurious facilities and resources. Many provide students with laptops, expensive sports equipment, and school trips. Unfortunately, well-equipped classrooms and technology infrastructure largely tell you nothing about the quality of the education provided by the school.

In my experience, fancy buildings don't make a difference when it comes to quality education. Some of my kids' best learning experiences took place at a kitchen table reading *Chaucer*, in church basements presenting at speech competitions, and in empty lots collecting prairie dog bones.

Microschools are a great example of this. If you could choose for your student to be one of two thousand children enrolled in a 35-million-dollar school or one of ten children in a micro school that meets with a dedicated teacher somewhere humble, which would you choose? These aren't easy decisions, but when you understand your priorities, the options narrow.

## *Extracurricular Activities*

Extracurricular activities are more than just an additional line on a college application — they can be a transformative part of your child's education and preparation for the future. As you evaluate schools and educational options, take note of the availability and diversity of extracurricular opportunities. This includes sports, arts, clubs, and community service initiatives that can enrich your child's learning experience and social development.

However, don't feel like you need to find a perfect, holistic education for your children in one place. For example, when my son was a sophomore, he navigated a blend of educational environments. He enrolled in four classes at the local district high school, a requirement that enabled him to compete on the swim team, as per Nebraska state regulations. Concurrently, he pursued computer science courses at a nearby college and engaged in an English curriculum I taught at home. This approach allowed him to experience the camaraderie of the swim team while continuing to be academically challenged in other subjects.

In addition to school-based offerings, many communities host recreation leagues and classes that can enrich a child's development in music, art, physical education, and more. With the rising trend in homeschooling, options for group activities outside of traditional school settings have expanded as well. From homeschool choirs to debate and speech leagues, there are increasingly diverse opportunities for social and educational engagement.

Moreover, some schools specialize in certain extracurricular programs. You may find a performing arts charter school in your area or a private institution with a nationally recognized robotics club. These focused environments not only foster passion and skill in a particular area but can also help your child explore interests that might inform their college major or even lay the foundation for a fulfilling career.

This is all to say, the goal is to meet your child's needs. Some institutions will align seamlessly with your child's educational and extracurricular interests and goals, and some will only get them partway there. By considering the spectrum of extracurricular opportunities — both within and beyond the school setting — you can help cultivate a rich, rewarding, and personalized educational journey for your child.

## *Parent Involvement and Communication*

Since you've picked up this book, it's likely that you are seeking an active role in your child's education—a commendable and influential position. The key question is: does your child's school welcome your involvement, or merely tolerate it?

When you meet with administrators, teachers, or counselors at potential schools, gauge their receptivity to parental engagement. Do you feel treated as a valued member of the educational team or more like an unwelcome observer?

It's important to note that 'parental involvement' can vary significantly from school to school. For instance, at one of the schools my children attended, parents were strongly encouraged to participate—but mainly in the context of fundraisers. Beyond this, the school appeared indifferent to parental input on educational matters.

Parental involvement, however, can be a critical component of a child's success. Being informed about what's happening at school equips you to support homework efforts at home, guide your children through interpersonal issues, and set and monitor academic goals. Essentially, it bridges the gap between the school environment and the home, enabling more consistent and effective support for the child.

Consider Merianne Jensen, whose children attend district public schools in Virginia. She has consistently maintained a presence in her children's schools. "I've always been involved," she said. "I was a room mom; I helped in the library so I could see what books were out there." When the school implemented contentious COVID-19 policies, her existing relationships with teachers and administrators proved invaluable. Merianne had established rapport and credibility, enabling her to secure her children with mask mandate exemptions and to stay informed about other policies, such as those concerning Social Emotional Learning (SEL), which we explored in Chapter 7.

In essence, choose a school that not only welcomes but values parental involvement and input. In such an environment, your role as a parent will be more respected. Hopefully, you'll be seen as a partner with the school in the pursuit of your child's educational success. After all, education is most effective when it is a collaborative effort between teachers, students, and parents.

In this collaborative model, you are not merely a spectator in your child's educational journey. You are an integral part of the team—contributing insights, supporting your children's unique needs, and ensuring that the education they receive aligns with your family's values and aspirations.

### *Location and Logistics*

States mandate the number of days students must spend in school per year, ranging from 160 in Colorado to 180 in Oklahoma, New York, Utah, and many other states. That's a lot of time, so it's wise to consider practical factors such as the school's location, transportation options, and daily schedule. Assess whether the school's location is convenient for your family and whether transportation arrangements align with your needs. Additionally, consider the school's schedule, including start and end times, breaks, and extracurricular activity timings, to ensure they mesh with your family's routine.

Many families discovered during covid shutdowns that school doesn't have to be an all-day affair. If your family runs a business or travels a lot, or if your kids have other time-consuming pursuits, you might want to consider a schooling option with maximum flexibility, like online school or homeschool.

### *Cost and Affordability*

The covid shutdowns may have been a disaster for children's educations—this is an understatement—but they went a long way toward speeding up the adoption of school choice policies across the country.

And because states have been passing programs like Education Savings Accounts (ESAs), vouchers, and tax-credit scholarships, schools that used to be too expensive for many parents are now within reach.

Only the wealthy had real school choice for many decades. The rest of us had to send our kids to the local public schools (which often cost much more than private school). In Nebraska, for example, taxpayers spend more than $15,000 on each child's public education each year. Meanwhile, the average private school tuition bill is $4,347. States like Arizona are allowing parents to direct some of their children's per pupil funding to any qualifying school, and new options like microschools are blossoming as a result. And after the 2023 state legislative sessions, several more states have followed suit. In Utah, parents can direct $8,000 to the school of their choice.

Research the options you can afford—you might be surprised that your child qualifies for more than just district public school.

### *Parent and student feedback*

I first learned about charter schools from a family we went to church with—way back in 1998. Other parents are often your best source of information about schools and education options. These are people with on-the-street experience, whose children have gone through programs and come out the other side. You can learn about how the kids fared during the next stage of their education journeys. Other parents can tell you which teachers to request and which to avoid. Parents can talk about different curricula, learning styles, and extra-curriculars.

Talk with your neighbors and friends and learn all you can as you explore your education options. Ultimately, the right school for your child will depend on their unique needs, interests, and talents. By carefully considering these factors and actively engaging with the school community, parents can make a well-informed decision that sets their child on a successful educational journey.

## Summary

- Focus on academic quality.
- The teaching staff matters.
- Pay attention to the school culture and values.
- Put school buildings and resources in proper perspective.
- How much do extracurricular activities matter to your children?
- Does the school invite parental involvement? How are the communications?
- Location and logistics can have a big impact on your lifestyle.
- Cost and affordability must be sustainable for your family's financial well-being.
- Talk with family and friends about their experiences at various schools.

## Go Deeper

Instead of reading articles or watching YouTube videos about schools in your area, pick up your phone and make some appointments for tours. Even if your child is still a couple of years away from kindergarten, start getting a feel for the academic options in your area. You might be surprised to find that different schools have very different atmospheres and philosophies. And the contrasts aren't often apparent unless you step foot inside the buildings and start talking to people. Don't be shy. You're not afraid to walk into a store to see what they offer. Walk into schools with the same kind of curiosity and confidence. Shopping around is a thousand times more important for your child's education than it is for a new pair of jeans.

# Part III - Paideia

# Chapter 13

# Preserving Western Civilization

Once upon a time, in the ancient city of Athens, there lived a renowned philosopher named Plato. He had established a school of philosophy known as the Academy, which was more than just a center of learning. It was a sanctuary for those who sought to explore the depths of the human mind and the nature of reality.

One day, a young student named Demetrius approached Plato, eager to become his disciple. Demetrius was intrigued by the stories he had heard about the Academy and Plato's teachings. Plato, always keen to assess the potential of his students, posed a question to Demetrius.

"Tell me, Demetrius," Plato began, "what do you think is the most important aspect of education?"

Demetrius pondered the question and then replied, "I believe that the pursuit of virtue is the most crucial goal of education. It is through cultivating virtuous qualities that one can lead a meaningful and fulfilling life."

Plato nodded, acknowledging Demetrius' response. "You have expressed a noble perspective, my young friend," he said. "Virtue is indeed a cornerstone of education. However, let me share with you a parable to illustrate the nature of learning."

Plato began to narrate the tale of "The Cave." He described a group of individuals who had spent their entire lives chained inside a dark cave, facing a wall. Behind them was a fire, and between the fire and the prisoners, puppeteers moved objects that cast shadows on the wall. These shadows were the prisoners' only perception of reality.

"Imagine," Plato continued, "if one of these prisoners were to break free from their chains and venture outside the cave. At first, the bright sunlight would blind them, and they would be bewildered by the real world that lay beyond. Gradually, as their eyes adjusted, they would come to realize the true nature of the world and the shadows they had mistaken for reality."

Demetrius listened intently, captivated by the allegory and its implications. When Plato concluded, he turned to Demetrius and asked, "What do you think this story tells us about education?"

Demetrius thought for a moment and replied, "It seems to suggest that education is not merely about acquiring knowledge but also about transcending our limited perspectives and seeking a deeper understanding of the world."

Plato smiled. "Precisely, Demetrius. Education is the journey of freeing ourselves from the chains of ignorance and recognizing the higher truths that exist beyond the shadows. It involves nurturing both the intellect and the soul, cultivating virtue, and striving for wisdom."

With these words, Plato welcomed Demetrius into the Academy. Under Plato's guidance, Demetrius and many others would come to understand that education was not a passive accumulation of facts but a dynamic process of enlightenment, reflection, and growth—a process that would shape their lives and impact the world for generations to come.

Western civilization was built on ideas like these—that each individual has the capacity to venture outside the cave and see clearly for himself. Tyrants don't like western civilization. They prefer life in the sunlight while the peons remain in the cave, ignorant of their own capacity. From Covid lockdowns to Netflix-binging, there seem to be so many ways for today's tyrants to keep us focused on shadows, unaware of the bright sunlight outside.

## Striving for ideals

The search for ideals runs like a thread through western civilization. Paideia starts from an ideal, and the goal of education was to help people rise above the dark shadows in the cave.

What has western civilization given to the world? The following is a short list:

### *Democracy*

The ancient Greeks established the foundations of democracy in Athens, which later influenced political systems around the world.

### *Scientific Advancements*

Pioneering figures like Isaac Newton, Galileo Galilei, Nicolaus Copernicus, and Albert Einstein revolutionized our understanding of the natural world and laid the groundwork for modern scientific methodologies and discoveries.

### *Rule of Law*

The western legal tradition, influenced by Roman law and later refined during the Enlightenment, has emphasized the principles of the rule of law, individual rights, and due process.

Concepts like habeas corpus, the presumption of innocence, and the separation of powers have significantly shaped legal systems worldwide.

### *Human Rights*

Western civilization has played a pivotal role in promoting the concept of human rights. Influential documents such as the Magna Carta (1215) and the Declaration of Independence (1776) have contributed to the recognition and protection of fundamental rights and liberties.

### *Cultural and Artistic Contributions*

Western civilization has produced a wealth of artistic and cultural achievements. From classical sculptures and Renaissance paintings to literature, music, and architecture, western cultures have enriched the world with masterpieces and creative expressions that continue to inspire and captivate.

### *Technological Innovations*

Western civilization has been at the forefront of technological advancements that have shaped the modern world. Developments like the Industrial Revolution, the invention of the printing press, electricity, the steam engine, computers, and the internet have transformed society, communication, and industry.

### *Economic Systems*

Western civilization has played a significant role in the development of various economic systems, including capitalism.

Capitalism, with its emphasis on private property rights, free markets, and entrepreneurship, has been instrumental in driving innovation, economic growth, and prosperity around the world.

Look around. The incredible world we inhabit was built by western civilization. Why, then, do we hear constant complaining and dismissal of its incomparable achievements? Mainly, the philosophies, ideals, and structures of western civilization uphold the sovereignty of the individual. Men and women are accountable to God first, not the state first. Those in power don't want people to be sovereign. They want power over us.

That's why western civilization is constantly maligned in K-12 public schools and universities. And that's why we need to resurrect the concept of paideia.

Today's obsession with racial and gender identity is at odds with the concept of paideia. Back in 4th century BC Athens, the idea of "Greekness" arose as a cultural ideal, not a description of someone's descent. The famous orator Isocrates said that the name "'Hellenes' suggests no longer a race but an intelligence, and the title 'Hellenes' is applied rather to those who share our culture [the Greek term used here is "paideusis," a term related to "paideia"] than to those who share a common blood."[52]

The United States of America embodies western civilization in many ways, and the term "American" is used much the way "Hellenes" was used in the fourth century BC. People don't have to look a certain way or even speak English to call themselves Americans. Immigrants in every generation come to America because they believe in the ideals of western civilization. They want their children to grow up in a place where they can count on the rule of law, participate in free markets, and engage in democracy.

But things have been falling apart around us in recent years, in large part because children are not being trained in their culture. They don't understand the blessings and benefits of western civilization, and they're not taught to be responsible citizens and heirs of their societies. They're not being taught the ideals and skills necessary to be free.

## Freedom

The word "freedom" gets co-opted by all kinds of organizations and propaganda machines because who doesn't like freedom? But what does it really mean to be free?

Indeed, the concept of freedom is deeply entwined with the kind of education one receives. Paideia, in the classical sense, aims not only to equip students with practical skills but to cultivate their character, intellect, and moral understanding of the world. It strives to produce individuals who are free not in the sense of unrestrained behavior, but in the sense of being able to govern oneself wisely and justly, to think critically and independently, and to contribute positively to the community. Here's a more detailed breakdown of what such an education aims to achieve:

### *Freedom of thought and expression*

A rich and expansive vocabulary, along with training in effective communication, empowers people to express themselves clearly, accurately, and beautifully. Linguistic skills also help children to understand others' perspectives more deeply, thereby fostering genuine dialogue and engagement with different ideas.

### *Moral freedom*

Paideia involves the cultivation of virtue and the development of a moral compass. This means that individuals are not slaves to their base desires or destructive habits, but are capable of acting in accordance with principles of justice, kindness, and integrity. They have the inner resources to make ethical decisions, even when those decisions are challenging.

### *Intellectual freedom*

A classically educated person is trained in various domains of knowledge—from the sciences to the humanities. This broad education enables individuals to approach problems from multiple angles and to continue learning throughout their lives. They have the freedom to change careers, to engage deeply with various kinds of work and study, and to adapt to new circumstances.

### *Civic freedom*

Classical education traditionally includes the study of political philosophy, history, and rhetoric. These skills prepare students to engage in civic life as informed and thoughtful citizens who can understand and critique various forms of governance and policy. They are not easily manipulated by propaganda or demagoguery, and they have the tools to advocate for just and wise policies.

### *Freedom from manipulation and tyranny*

A grounding in rhetoric and logic equips individuals to recognize when they are being manipulated or deceived, whether by political actors, advertisers, or anyone else. They can discern the difference between rational arguments and fallacies, between evidence-based conclusions and baseless claims.

Classically educated people are free from tyranny, from those who want to persuade them (either to join their political ideology or to buy a particular brand of detergent). Having studied rhetoric, they spot fallacies, inconsistencies, and deception.

### *Personal freedom*

By cultivating inner virtues such as self-control, resilience, and introspection, individuals are empowered to lead fulfilling, purposeful lives. They are not solely reliant on external circumstances for their happiness but have cultivated a rich inner life that allows for contentment and personal growth regardless of external conditions.

In sum, paideia aims for a kind of freedom that is rich and multi-dimensional—it is the freedom to live a good, meaningful, and effective life, both for oneself and for one's community. This vision of freedom is far more meaningful than just license to do whatever you want. It is freedom grounded in wisdom, virtue, and deep understanding.

## Paideia

Paideia is a Greek term that encompasses the concept of education and the overall development of an individual. It refers to the holistic education of a person, involving intellectual, moral, and physical aspects. The term derives from the Greek word "paideuo," which means "to educate" or "to bring up." Paideia is the power of building culture intentionally. It helps people answer questions like these:

Where did we come from?
How do we think?
What do we eat?

Do we spend our time productively?
Do we value God's creations?
Do we have large families? Small families?
How do we interact with each other?
Do we value honesty? Do we respect others' property?

Millions of questions like these are transmitted through culture, and if the culture is to be maintained, it must be taught to children.

Cultures worldwide have developed meaningful ways to transmit their stories, myths, customs, and norms to the younger generation, thus perpetuating the culture into the future. Cherokee author Brad Wagnon writes children's books that re-tell traditional foundational stories of his heritage. For example, his book *The Land of the Great Turtles* explains a Cherokee creation story about a beautiful island with everything the people could need. The Creator tasks the people with caring for the animals, but the children decide to play with the turtles instead of tending to their responsibilities. Stories like this teach morals, perpetuate culture, and give children a sense of belonging to something bigger than themselves.

In addition to telling stories, many cultures use music and dance to introduce children to their heritage. In Romania, schoolchildren learn a dance called "Alunelul," which means "little hazelnut." Dancers stand in a circle with their hands on each other's shoulders and complete the steps in unison. As they dance, they sing:

Hazelnut, hazelnut, come let's dance and be happy.
He (or she) who dances will grow strong and tall,
He (or she) who doesn't will stay tiny and small.
Hazelnut, . . . Dance, oh dance on this spot until the grass grows,
dance, oh dance, never stop or slow down.

Like the Cherokee story, this cultural piece of folklore brings people together and even offers a moral: if you get up and dance, you'll be healthier!

Sadly, there's been a concerted effort in America and other western nations to suppress our cultural inheritance. Today, many kids are unfamiliar with Aesop's fables, traditional fairy tales, the Virginia Reel, Johnny Appleseed, and even Paul Revere. Instead of squandering our cultural inheritance, we must strengthen it and pass it on.

In ancient Greece, the educational ideal of paideia was not limited to formal schooling but extended to the broader cultural and social environment. It emphasized the importance of learning through engagement with the arts, participation in public life, and exposure to ethical and philosophical teachings. The goal was to shape individuals into knowledgeable, virtuous, and active members of society.

In the Greek text of Ephesians 6:4, the word used for "nurture" is "παιδεία" (paideia). It is derived from the same root word "pais" that gives rise to the concept of paideia, which we discussed earlier. In this context, "paideia" can be understood as encompassing the broader idea of training, discipline, and instruction.

So, in Ephesians 6:4, when it says, "bring them up in the training and instruction of the Lord," the Greek word "paideia" carries the meaning of nurturing, educating, and providing guidance to children within the framework of the teachings and principles of the Lord.

Ancient Greeks and Romans understood that civilizations don't just continue unless you prepare children to be the stewards of what their fathers built. Early Christians used the same word to speak about how to raise children. People in the Middle Ages and Renaissance used the classical education model built on paideia, and the Victorians still clung to remnants of paideia.

But paideia has been so thoroughly forgotten in our modern world, that most of us have never seen the word. And it shows. We now have multiple generations that received passable basic academic skills or vocational training but very little of the kind of education that makes us free, that makes us proud of our heritage, and that helps us to see our fellow humans as divine beings with limitless potential. If we don't re-adopt paideia, there won't be much left to preserve.

## Summary

- Western civilization is well-worth preserving. It has given us the amazing world we live in today.
- Classical education helps people maintain their freedom in many different areas.
- Paideia will help Western Civilization endure.

### Go Deeper

Klavan, Spencer. *How to Save the West: Ancient Wisdom for 5 Modern Crises.* Regnery, 2023.

Spencer Klavan is a classicist with a Ph.D. from Oxford and a deep understanding of Western Civilization. He alleges that the situation is dire, but every crisis we face today, we have faced before. If you enjoy *How to Save the West*, you'll probably also like listening to his podcast, *Young Heretics*, where you can listen to interviews and learn about "truth, beauty, and the stuff that matters."

## Chapter 14

# Norms and Culture

Sometimes, when I feel discouraged about the state of the world, I watch old movies, especially from the 1940s. Although these films were created decades before I was born, they make me feel nostalgic. The characters seem to live in a world with coherent norms, comforting routines, and civil discourse. No one wore sweatpants to the grocery store, and people knew the mailman's name. In some ways, it feels like our society is a complex jigsaw puzzle that has fallen off the card table and spilled onto the floor. While the overall image remains in my mind, the pieces lie scattered — disconnected, jumbled at awkward angles, creating puzzling gaps.

Generations have unfolded with people navigating life without formal, or even informal, lessons on living well. Dinner used to be a predictable event with the whole family sitting down together at 5:00 on the dot, but now it often feels more like a race than a ritual. Traditions that once shaped the way we dress, dine, communicate with our neighbors, and resolve our disputes, seem to have quietly slipped away.

Now, as parents, the compass we use to guide our children feels like it's missing a needle. Whether you opt for homeschooling or a traditional classroom setting for your children's education, the vital element remains the same: an environment that instills not just knowledge, but culture and norms as well.

This is not an insignificant matter. Trying to preserve the traditions and norms of our culture is like trying to rebuild a classic car without ever having driven one. Many of us were not brought up with explicit training in manners, norms, or traditions, yet here we are, tasked with passing down a legacy we haven't fully inherited ourselves. But it's a task of undeniable importance, a cornerstone in constructing a fulfilling, mindful life for the next generation.

It's time to ignite a renaissance in American culture and learning. So, how do we piece that incredible puzzle back together?

## Virtue doesn't happen by chance

Civilizations are like sandcastles, complicated but fragile. And societies can lose their way, as we're all too aware. This has been quietly unfolding in our modern American society for several decades, but history is full of similar stories from around the world.

In Northern Italy in the fifteenth century, people craved change (not unlike our current moment in the West). Citizens gathered on piazzas to discuss revolutionary ideas. They wanted to re-stabilize and rejuvenate their society, and education was central to these conversations. Vittorino da Feltre started a school, which he called "La Giocosa," which means "The Pleasant House" (a lovely name for a school). Here, students from all walks of life — from royalty to the poor chosen for their potential — were welcomed into an educational family.[53] Da Feltre, whose work is often credited with revitalizing classical education in Northern Italy, was a stalwart believer that virtue could be taught (a torch he carried from Plato). As he put it, "Not everyone is obliged to excel in philosophy, medicine, or the law, nor are all equally favored by nature; but all are destined to live in society and to practice virtue."[54]

It's true: all are destined to live in society and to practice virtue. Sadly, we have far too many examples of what happens when children learn from teachers who feel no obligation to teach morals and ethics.

In Chapter 8, I discussed Jackson Hedrick, the teacher who went to prison for sexually abusing a student at my children's middle school. I want to briefly revisit that story from another point of view.

Jackson Hedrick was 22 years old when he was arrested, just 7 months into his first teaching job after graduating from college. A hometown boy, he had grown up in the neighborhood where he landed his first teaching job and had earned his degree right there in Lincoln at the University of Nebraska.

Having raised children in Lincoln myself, I can tell you that "virtue" is not a term students often hear at school. Shortly after Hedrick's arrest, while school administrators and local journalists scrambled to distance themselves from the situation, Marjorie Kostelnik, Dean of UNL's College of Education and Human Sciences, told a journalist, "It's very rare that these incidents happen. But whenever we hear that someone is believed to have failed in their professional and ethical code of conduct, we're always very disappointed and concerned."

A "professional and ethical code of conduct" does not sound strong enough to guide the behavior of people who work with children. Those terms sound sterile and superficial, like a cheaply printed mission statement that hangs on the wall but is never read by the people it's supposed to guide. A professional and ethical code of conduct is a poor excuse for virtue, which is an unshakable knowledge of right and wrong. Kostelnik's "disappointment and concern" don't seem adequate as a response for what happened to Jackson Hedrick.[55]

Postmodern relativity saturates many schools today, and talking about right and wrong is considered a micro aggression—or worse. But failing to teach virtue is downright cruel.

Five years post-arrest, Hedrick died while in custody, marking a somber end to a story that left lives irrevocably marred. How many children have to lose their way because adults are unwilling to teach them about virtue?

Samuel Johnson, an eminent scholar of the eighteenth century, said that scientific knowledge was not the great or frequent business of the human mind. Instead, "the first requisite is the religious and moral knowledge of right and wrong, the next is an acquaintance with the history of mankind, and with those examples which may be said to embody truth, and prove by events the reasonableness of opinions." In other words, we should spend great effort helping children learn the virtues they'll need in everyday life. He feared that education was turning away from "'religious and moral knowledge' into the cold embrace of the 'knowledge of external nature.'" Today, most students spend their entire K-12 years (and often college, too) in the cold embrace of knowledge that seems displaced from virtue. Is it any wonder they struggle?

## Teach kids to be classy

In 1955, Esther "Eppie" Lederer launched a newspaper column that became an iconic part of American life. Also known as Ann Landers, Eppie became a trusted voice on all things related to manners and personal challenges. In fact, her words and wisdom became such a mainstay that she continued writing the column until 2002, the year she passed away at age 83.

One of her most cherished columns focuses on a topic that seems increasingly elusive today: what it means to have class. In it, she defines class not as a matter of wealth or style, but as a deep-seated grace, a compassion for others, and a willingness to accept responsibility for your actions. It's about holding your head high without looking down on others.

> Class never runs scared. It is sure-footed and confident, and it can handle whatever comes along.
> Class has a sense of humor. It knows that a good laugh is the best lubricant for oiling the machinery of human relations.
> Class knows that good manners are nothing more than a series of small sacrifices and minor inconveniences.
> Class bespeaks an aristocracy unrelated to ancestors or money. Some extremely wealthy people have no class at all, while others who are struggling to make ends meet are loaded with it.
> Class is real. You can't fake it.
> Class is comfortable in its own skin. It never puts on airs.
> Class never tries to build itself up by tearing others down.
> Class is already up and need not attempt to look better by making others look worse.
> Class can "walk with kings and keep its virtue and talk with crowds and keep the common touch." Everyone is comfortable with the person who has class because he is comfortable with himself.
> If you have class, you've got it made. If you don't have class, no matter what else you have, it won't make up for it.

Obviously, no one is born with class. It must be learned, and you, as a parent, can train your children to have the good manners and make the "small sacrifices and minor inconveniences" that will help them feel comfortable around kings and commoners alike.

As you do, your own home life will improve. It might even feel like Vittorino da Feltre's "Pleasant House." And your children will be welcomed and wanted everywhere they go.

## Mr. and Mrs.

Sometime in the last fifty or sixty years, adults stopped requiring children to use the terms Mr. and Mrs. (or Ms.). This might seem like a small, insignificant point, but it makes a substantial difference. I didn't grow up calling my adult neighbors Mr. Warfield and Ms. Potter. When my parents talked about them with me, they said "Carlos" and "Lynn."

Fortunately, when my kids were small, we lived next to a family who taught their children to use Mr. and Mrs. for adults. We adopted the norm, and I'm so grateful for it. Although they may not realize it, children respect adults more when they call them Mr. Miller. There's a distance between them, and this is right and appropriate.

Also, it's important to teach kids that *all* adults deserve this respect. When kids refer to the school janitor as Mr. Wilson and the principal as Mrs. Fellini, they're internalizing the idea that all people deserve respect, regardless of the kind of work they do.

And when children finally earn the title of Mr. or Ms. themselves, they feel proud. They are now members of society on which younger people can depend.

## Manners

Does your children's school teach them how to be classy? In addition to "please" and "thank you," do students learn how to make introductions, apologies, and invitations? Of course, this kind of training should begin at home before children ever show up at school, but you don't want all of your hard work to be undone in an environment that cares nothing for manners.

If you're like many American adults, you didn't receive as much manners training as you'd have liked. Instead of worrying, just learn it along with your kids. Practice etiquette together and help everyone to make improvements.

For a while when we homeschooled, I used etiquette books to reset bad behavior. If a child misbehaved, I'd assign him or her to copy down a few paragraphs from a large etiquette book I picked up at a thrift store. Sometimes another person's authority adds to the lesson, and it never hurts to practice handwriting, right?

## Family Traditions

Over the past few generations, families have become fractured and distant, and in this process, traditions have disappeared. If this has happened in your family, don't feel that traditions have been irrevocably lost. You can restart old traditions and establish new ones.

Traditions help children feel secure. They provide a sense of pride, identity, and security. Traditions can be large or small. They can happen once a year on a specific holiday, or they can happen every night at bedtime.

If your child's school denigrates your family traditions (or your country's traditions), it's time to look for a new school.

## Community Traditions

One year, our family was in Spain during Holy Week, and we couldn't believe the spirit of unity we witnessed during the processions and celebrations leading up to Easter. In the United States, it's rare to find a community with such high participation rates in festivals and celebrations, and in many schools, there seems to be a concerted effort to abolish traditions.

One of my kids' schools had a tradition of decorating classroom doors during the week before Christmas vacation. The class with the best-decorated door would get a pizza party on the last day before break. The one year my kids attended this school, the students had the option of choosing between two different themes: winter and recycling.

In the season when children were giddy with excitement over Christmas and Hannukah, they were expected to get excited about cold weather or trash? It was one of the last straws for me. Over the break, I enrolled my kids in an online charter school. Not only were the academics iffy at this school, but they clearly had an agenda. Ignoring and disparaging community traditions breaks society down. It makes people feel isolated, lonely, and rootless.

In essence, traditions are the church bells that call a community together. They remind us that we are part of something larger than ourselves and that we can call on familiar rituals and celebrations to guide us through life.

## Church

"Separation of church and state" has become a sort of mantra in American education, but it's almost always used incorrectly or in the wrong context. It's true that the state shouldn't force children to adopt a certain religion, but religion shouldn't be barred from education.

Paideia includes moral training as well as intellectual training, and religion is the fountain of morality. Parents who help their children integrate into a religious community create a solid network for their kids. A strong faith community is like a laboratory for learning how to live a good and decent life.

Our religious community provides a scripture-study class for high school-aged kids. Called "seminary," this class typically meets before school, around 6:00 a.m., five days a week. Our kids developed a solid understanding of the scriptures and built relationships with other like-minded students. Although getting them up in the morning was not easy, they grew from the sacrifices they made to learn about their religion and build their moral foundation.

Churches have always been centers of learning. Some people today try to perpetuate a stereotype equating religiosity with ignorance, but it doesn't ring true. It's not true. Religions foster the idea that there is order in the world, and therefore, the world is knowable. If the world is knowable, education has a purpose, and there's great satisfaction in learning.

## Summary

- Virtue is an essential component of education—does your children's school agree?
- Teach kids to be classy.
- Insist on addressing adults as Mr. and Mrs.
- Practice good manners at home, emphasizing that manners aren't superficial; they're a way of making sure everyone around you feels respected and valued.
- Focus on establishing and maintaining traditions in your home and community.
- Church—every institution has a religion. Does your child's school respect yours?

### Go Deeper

I have two suggestions for going deeper in this area. One is not very deep, and the other one might require scuba gear.

First, for the not-too-deep. Find an etiquette book you like and read through it. Some of the tips will seem quaint and even silly, but you'll start to think about the way you live and interact with others. Here's a fun one:

Carlin, Lesley and Honore McDonough Ervin. *Things You Need to Be Told: A Handbook for Polite Behavior in a Tacky, Rude World!* Berkley, 2001.

Second, *Norms & Nobility* is deep but incredibly fascinating. Hicks argues that the true purpose of education is to nurture the soul and cultivate a sense of nobility, helping students to become morally upright and thoughtful individuals. It's not a long book, but you can't whip through it while you monitor the kids on the playground.

Hicks, David. *Norms & Nobility*. Praeger, 1981.

## Chapter 15

# Old School Academic Traditions

*We dole out lip-service to the importance of education — lip-service and, just occasionally, a little grant of money; we post-pone the school leaving-age, and plan to build bigger and better schools; the teachers slave conscientiously in and out of school-hours, till responsibility becomes a burden and a nightmare; and yet, as I believe, all this devoted effort is largely frustrated, because we have lost the tools of learning, and in their absence can only make a botched and piecemeal job of it.*

We have lost the tools of learning. Many of us would agree with that statement today, but Dorothy Sayers made this pronouncement in 1947. 1947! Sayers was one of the first women to graduate from Oxford University, and she went on to write sixteen novels, ten plays, six translations, and twenty-four works of non-fiction. The above quote comes from a famous speech she delivered at Oxford to faculty and students. Called "The Lost Tools of Learning," Sayers' speech is a call-to-action, an impassioned plea for a return to old-school academic traditions.

Why don't schools stick to tried-and-true teaching methods and traditions? For one, university professors in education departments must continually develop and publish new theories and methodologies to achieve tenure and advance their careers. They teach these new theories to students who become teachers, and districts adopt them. Also, American K-12 has been in a downward, damage-control spiral for decades now. As we saw in Chapter 7, legislators and bureaucrats change regulatory requirements every few years, cementing their legacy and attempting to rescue the system from itself. Additionally, states change their standardized tests regularly so people can't compare today's outcomes with those of a few years ago.

But details about state reporting and standardized tests aren't the primary concern for parents. What we really want is for our kids to become capable, self-sufficient adults who can think for themselves. We want them to avoid the following problems described by Dorothy Sayers in "The Lost Tools of Learning":

> Have you ever, in listening to a debate among adult and presumably responsible people, been fretted by the extraordinary inability of the average debater to speak to the question, or to meet and refute the arguments of speakers on the other side? Or have you ever pondered upon the extremely high incidence of irrelevant matter which crops up at committee meetings, and upon the very great rarity of persons capable of acting as chairmen of committees? And when you think of this, and think that most of our public affairs are settled by debates and committees, have you ever felt a certain sinking of the heart?

If we stick to the tried-and-true, we're less likely to experience that "sinking of the heart." In this chapter, we'll look at some old school academic traditions that have proven effective for many generations of students—and will probably work for your kids, too.

## Cursive

Thirteen-year-old Taija Morales received an assignment from Fountain Middle School to "learn a family tradition." She asked her grandma Debbie Younger for her Salad Dressing Cake recipe. Grandma happily handed over her handwritten 3x5 index card and Taija said, "This is in cursive, and I don't know how to read cursive."[57]

Why didn't Taija know how to read cursive? Her school, like most other public schools in the United States, no longer taught the skill. Public schools are notorious for adopting methodologies and programs before they've been vetted or proven. The latest-and-greatest is just too tempting. And as they adopt SEL and other pseudo-academic programs, they drop the classics like cursive, rhetoric and speaking, geography, and more. When you take control of your kids' education, you can ensure that they learn foundational skills that modern educators have deemed unimportant.

Does it matter whether a child can write in cursive? In the digital age, does it make sense to spend time on this handwriting skill?

Taija's inability to read her grandmother's recipe illustrates a problem: the lack of cursive knowledge cuts children off from the past. They can't read the original Declaration of Independence, handwritten recipes, or birthday cards from their grandparents. And in severing these ties, children are left adrift, bereft of the traditions, family ties, and culture that helps them feel at home in their own society.

The major break in cursive instruction took place in 2009 with the release of the Common Core state standards initiative.

The standards didn't require the teaching of cursive or even suggest teaching it. So many states and school districts abandoned cursive altogether.

After all, schools have taken on so many non-academic responsibilities, and it's difficult to fit everything into a school day. In 2009 (the same year the Common Core standards excluded cursive writing), Vi Supon wrote the following in the *Journal of Instructional Psychology*: "Teacher education programs now have the demands of courses for inclusion, technology, diversity, and ESL/ELL students, in addition to the content major. Hence, writing is often not required."[58]

The trend was clear, and it had been picking up steam. In 2004, David Rufo wrote, "Why do we force our children to write in a systemized loopy script that is rather difficult to decipher and leaves many adults with knots the size of walnuts on their knuckles?"[59] Well, when you put it that way, why indeed? Cursive sounds barbaric, maybe abusive, right? So kids stopped learning cursive, and teachers stopped learning how to teach both printed handwriting and cursive.

Kathleen Wright, founder and executive director of the Handwriting Collaborative said she can walk into a room of 100 teachers and ask how many of them have received any kind of instruction on how to teach handwriting. About 5 of the 100 will raise their hands, and they're typically the oldest teachers in the room.

"Handwriting is a fine-motor skill and it requires direct instruction," she said. And our society has been devaluing handwriting for so long that many teachers seem hostile to it. "My granddaughter, who is 18, took a note to one of her teachers," Wright said, "and the teacher handed it back and said, 'I don't read cursive.'"

Is eschewing cursive a real issue? In a world dominated by screens, should we guide children towards typing instead? Surprisingly, handwriting, it turns out, has profound developmental impacts. FMRI (functional magnetic resonance imaging) studies of pre-literate children reveal that forming letters by hand—unlike typing on a keyboard or tapping a screen—significantly activates the brain's reading circuits. In the same news story that included Taijua Morales' story about her grandmother's cake recipe, KRDO talked to Colin Mullaney, Executive Director of The Vanguard School, where students start learning cursive in kindergarten.

"Students are learning to write in cursive at the same time they're learning to read. It tends to help students see words as...blocks of letters that have a beginning and an end," Mullaney said.

And so, cursive has begun reappearing in sectors where parental influence is greatest—in school choice schools. If you want to see what parents are after, look at what charter schools, private schools, homeschools, and microschools are doing. They can't exist unless they provide an education that parents want.

That said, if you want to start emphasizing handwriting and cursive, you'll need to start where your children are at.

### *Toddlers and preschoolers*

Kathleen Wright recommends getting kids off their iPads. "We used to get crayons and coloring paper when kids were bored in a restaurant—don't hand them a phone. You don't want to curtail fine-motor development."

At ages 3 and 4, you can start to do some fine motor work like stringing beads, using short crayons and pencils. Look for resources on the internet for fine motor activities. Start young with fun activities that can be done in 3-5 minutes. If parents have kids in kindergarten, have a conversation with the kindergarten teacher early on. Being a parent advocate in schools is huge. We don't want kids to hit 2nd or 3rd grade and have the teacher suggest that the child needs to see a specialist. That's not necessary if you start working on handwriting early on. If the school is using a particular instructional method, the parents should use the same method at home.

### *Early elementary school*

Wright recommends having a conversation with the child's teacher about handwriting. Don't automatically assume that there's a problem if the child is holding a pencil wrong. More likely, nobody showed the child how to hold a pencil. Model for your children. Let kids see you writing and reading. Your child needs to see that you are writing, and you value it.

### *3rd grade*

Third grade is the ideal time to learn cursive. Children's fine motor skills are developed enough to manage the task, and cursive consolidates the literacy skills they've gained over the past two or three years. It's harder to learn cursive later, just like it's harder to learn to ride a bike as an adult. But if they're motivated, students can certainly learn later on.

### *Older children (or adults!) learning cursive*

With motivation, older children and adults can learn cursive, too. It's easy to find online courses and workbooks, and you can watch YouTube videos about techniques and exercises.

Remember, children can't sign their names if they don't learn cursive. A document examiner told Kathleen Wright that it's easier to forge print than cursive. So take advantage of the early years, and give your kids the advantage of learning how to write beautifully.

## Rhetoric (Oratory)

Today's language arts programs focus mainly on reading and writing, and students rarely receive instruction in speaking. But in classical education, rhetoric, or the art of oratory and persuasion, was considered one of the three essential components of a well-rounded education. It involves the study of persuasive techniques, public speaking, composition, and presentation skills. Rhetoric aims to cultivate the ability to express ideas eloquently, engage an audience, and influence others through effective communication.

Today, with instant video communication via social media and Zoom, it seems that rhetoric skills are more important than ever. If you can't find a school that teaches rhetoric, consider including extracurricular activities like mock trial, speech, and debate.

In summary, rhetoric and oratory education extends far beyond the classroom, preparing students to be effective communicators, critical thinkers, and engaged citizens in an increasingly complex world. These are foundational skills that serve students in many ways throughout their lives.

## History/Geography

Social studies replaced history and geography a couple of generations ago in American K-12 public schools. The National Council for the Social Studies provides a definition of social studies that helps us understand why history and geography are out and social studies is in.

*"Social studies is the integrated study of the social sciences and humanities to promote civic competence. Within the school program, social studies provides coordinated, systematic study drawing upon such disciplines as anthropology, archaeology, economics, geography, history, law, philosophy, political science, psychology, religion, and sociology, as well as appropriate content from the humanities, mathematics, and natural sciences. The primary purpose of social studies is to help young people develop the ability to make informed and reasoned decisions for the public good as citizens of a culturally diverse, democratic society in an interdependent world."*

In other words, social studies is designed to shape young minds to accept a certain worldview, and the educators will use any subject matter necessary to do it.

As a subject, social studies treats students like cogs in factory machinery, not as fully developed human beings who can make their own decisions and steer their own futures. Make sure your children get History and Geography, not social studies. With a well-developed conception of the past and present, children will not be easily duped by people who simply want their votes and support.

The wonderful thing about abandoning social studies for the real deal is that history and geography are fascinating. And as students learn about the world and their relation to it, they gain essential perspective about current events. With a solid background in history and geography, children have the knowledge to shape their own world views and avoid viral mind traps.

## Music

Earlier in this chapter, we talked about the trivium (grammar, logic, and rhetoric), the foundational studies of a classical education. After mastering the trivium, students moved on to the quadrivium (astronomy, geometry, arithmetic, and music). Why would music be included as a necessary study?

The ancient Greeks viewed music as a part of mathematics and saw it as a representation of scientific and mathematical order in the universe. Music was seen as a study of aesthetics and beauty, incorporating principles such as form, proportion, and motion.

A classical study of music enables individuals to connect with beauty and appreciate its significance. Your children can study music history to gain a deeper understanding of aesthetics and its connection to broader historical contexts and participate in music through singing, playing instruments, and attending concerts, as these experiences provide insight into the hard work and accomplishment associated with beauty.

Many see music as a vital component of classical education, aligning with the principles of classical thinking and values. It promotes the exploration of beauty and its manifestation through music and the arts, emphasizing the richness that comes from understanding and embracing the cultural history and significance of music.

## Art

It's no secret that art has taken a nosedive in the past century. Italian writer and journalist Italo Calvino summed it up: "What is modern art but the attempt to pinpoint vague, incorporeal inexpressible sensations? What is modern art, I might add, but the most solemn pile of nonsense that ever appeared on earth?"[60]

If you agree with Calvino, you probably don't want your children wasting precious time on a "solemn pile of nonsense," especially when they're the inheritors of a vast treasure trove of art produced by thousands of years of western civilization.

Classical education views art as an essential component of a well-rounded education. It recognizes the value of artistic expression, creativity, and aesthetic appreciation in the development of individuals. Art is beautiful, and by studying it and producing it, children learn to appreciate the world around and within them.

And it's not just about creating art. Classical education often emphasizes the study of art history, exploring the works of renowned artists and their contributions to different periods and cultures. Elementary school students can be familiar with Raphael, Dürer, and Van Gogh. They can imitate the works of Claude Monet and Georgia O'Keefe. Through the study of art history, students gain a deeper understanding of the historical, cultural, and social contexts in which art is created, and they learn to appreciate the diverse forms, styles, and techniques employed by artists throughout history.

In the past, students learned to draw well, and in doing so, they learned to see God's creations in a new, more appreciative light. Students are encouraged to engage in hands-on artistic activities, such as drawing, painting, sculpture, and music, to cultivate their creative abilities and refine their technical skills. Through practice and artistic production, students gain a greater appreciation for the discipline, effort, and craftsmanship required in creating meaningful and aesthetically pleasing works of art.

When it comes to K-12 education, the latest and greatest just can't compete with the tried and true. Trust the fine-tuned discoveries made over thousands of years and give your children a foundation on which they can build.

## Summary

- Incorporate cursive into children's learning.
- Find ways to practice oratory.
- Choose history and geography over social studies.
- Add art and music to your kids' educations.

### Go Deeper

If you have young children at home, help them improve their fine motor skills and writing readiness. Kathleen S. Wright kindly shared her researched tips with me, which are included in the Appendix of this book.

# Chapter 16

# Don't Go It Alone

It's not fair. I mean, your great-grandmother sent her kids off to schools where they copied scripture verses to practice their handwriting and learned to love their country. I know because I have a notebook of my great-grandmother's school days, from about 1910. Growing up in small-town Illinois, she learned virtue at her public school.

But maybe it *is* fair. After all, you and I aren't living through the Depression. We're not sending our kids to the trenches of World War I. We have different battles. Our society is ailing morally, and we're bringing up children in a world that wants to steal their childhoods at every turn.

We have our own battles, and we can't lie down in defeat.

When you decide to take the reins of your children's educations and go against the grain, you need support. So don't go it alone. Use the people and resources around you for encouragement and day-to-day help.

## Family Cooperation

Parents are not the only people losing sleep over America's current education predicament. Many grandparents and aunts and uncles find themselves wringing their hands over what they hear about public schools today. They want to do something to help, but they often feel helpless.

Take advantage of family members who want to help your children. This can be done in many ways. For instance, a woman in our neighborhood homeschooled her own three children as well as her niece. To compensate for the education labor, the mother of the niece pitched in additional funds to the homeschool and took care of some of the meals.

One single mother, Jenny, enlisted her parents, Chris and Sarah, to help with her children's education. Chris described the local option as "a failed school" and told me how much he enjoyed teaching his grandchildren. The couple divides and conquers, dividing the subjects based on their levels of comfort. Said Chris, "I can say that homeschooling is very good fun and sometimes challenging to my own knowledge and understanding."

Chris and Sarah's grandchildren get to spend their days with people who love them and are willing to sacrifice for them. And they're building relationships and memories they'll treasure all their lives.

Grandparents aren't the only family members who can lend a hand. Did you know that Khan Academy started out as one man tutoring his cousin?

In 2004, Sal Khan offered to help his cousin Nadia as she struggled with unit conversion in her math class. Nadia lived in New Orleans, and Sal lived in Boston, so the tutoring happened through the phone and Yahoo Doodle.

Sal was a good tutor, and before long, word got out. He started tutoring a handful of other cousins and nieces and nephews—so many, in fact, that it was taking up too much time. So he began recording videos and posting them to YouTube so all of his pupils could watch them at their own pace. Today,

Khan Academy content is watched by tens of millions of students all over the world.

Maybe you have a brother or aunt who could help your children via Zoom or FaceTime. Not only can you take advantage of the various strengths and talents of family members, but you'll strengthen relationships. The adults will be more invested in your children, and your kids will have mentors to look up to. Before the advent of factory-style government school, this is how families educated their kids.

Take Frank Lloyd Wright, for example. His two single aunts, Jane and Ellen Lloyd Jones, taught nieces and nephews as well as local children, giving them individual attention and encouraging their gifts. They called their school Hillside Home School.

The aunts noticed Frank's talents and asked him to design a building for their school. He was just nineteen years old at the time, but he took on the project. Not only was it successful, but it was an important steppingstone in his architecture career.

You never know how your family will benefit from asking for help with your children's education.

## Build your community

One of the biggest deterrents to choosing alternative schooling options is the unfamiliar social landscape. Traditional public schools relish their place as "the heart of the community." And kids who attend private schools, online schools, or homeschools might feel out of place in the neighborhood.

As school choice and homeschool expand, this is less and less of an issue. And even if you live in a place where nearly all the kids go to the same school, your kids don't have to feel alone or out of place.

Yes, you want your children to know and love the other kids in the neighborhood, but you also need a community of parents and children who share your perspective and, hopefully, your schedule.

When our kids were enrolled in an online charter school, we took advantage of school-wide field trips and events to get to know the other families in our area who also participated in the school. Once we knew each other, we could help each other with rides and arrange playdates and other social activities.

If you homeschool, join some local homeschool activities or co-ops so you can find out which other children are at home during school hours. Use church and extracurricular activities to build friendships and connections.

To maintain friendships and build community, plan regularly scheduled activities or playdates that you can depend on. Every third Thursday, for example, you can meet up with other homeschooling families at the park for lunch and playtime. Everyone looks forward to the interaction, and it's a great way to welcome new homeschoolers into the community.

## Enlist neighbors and friends

Acton Academy bills itself as "one-room schoolhouses" for the 21$^{st}$ century. With over 300 schools nationwide, the idea is growing. Students learn through daily Socratic discussions, self-directed projects, core academics, and apprenticeships.

How do students find the apprenticeships? They locate mentors in their local communities and ask for guidance (and ultimately an apprenticeship).

You might be surprised how willing your friends and neighbors are to mentor your children. Right now, you might have an older neighbor who would love to teach your kids to crochet or garden. Or your daughter might be interested in architecture, and an architect lives right down the street.

Our son loved to take things apart when he was little, and we had several neighbors who would bring over defunct appliances for him. He spent weeks taking apart a washing machine motor donated by a kind neighbor up the street.

You can only develop these kinds of relationships by getting to know the people around you. Host a block party or enlist all the neighbor kids to perform the Nativity at Christmas and invite the entire street. Not only will you have more friends and neighbors to help you teach your children, but you'll have a warmer, safer community—even after the kids have grown up.

## Celebrate successes together

Another benefit of building your community is that you have people to help you celebrate successes. The traditional district schools are pretty good at celebrating. They have teacher appreciation week, graduation, end-of-school parties, and festivals.

Use the community you build to provide similar celebrations for your kids and their friends. As your children achieve goals, throw parties for them. Host a homeschool graduation ceremony. Cheer the children on and support the other adults.

Raising the next generation is the most important work we do. Take time to praise your children for their hard work, and remember to pat yourself on the back, too. Heaven knows the education establishment won't pat your back for you.

In building your own educational community, you are crafting not only a support system but also a celebration squad, marking life's big and small achievements with the joy and recognition they deserve.

## Summary

- Increase family cooperation to help children succeed academically.
- Build a community of like-minded friends and neighbors.
- Enlist friends and neighbors to help with your kids' educations.
- Celebrate successes as a community.

### Go Deeper

Instead of researching more about this topic, make plans to start building your community. If you don't know where to start, try one of these ideas:

Reach out to family members and find out what concerns they have about education. You might be able to address your concerns together.

Plan a block party to get to know your neighbors.

Join an online forum that discusses K-12 education, schooling options, or parenting.

Talk to other families at church about education. If you don't currently attend a church, find a faith community.

# Chapter 17

# What Matters More?

Do you remember what it felt like to become a parent for the first time? I remember leaving the hospital with our firstborn baby, the weight of her tiny body against my chest and shoulder. How could something so small capture my heart so completely? We had driven to the hospital with just two of us. Now we were three, and the responsibility felt staggering. How could *we* be in charge of a tiny baby? I'd spent the last six months reading about babies and parenting, but that all seemed meaningless in the face of an actual, crying infant.

And what surprised me most of all was the fierce love I felt for this child. She was mine, and I would do anything for her. She spent the first month connected to a heart and breathing monitor as a result of complications from the pregnancy and delivery. Every now and then, the monitor beeped, and my heart stopped. I had to gently stir her to remind her to breathe.

Fortunately, she outgrew the problem, and she's been breathing well ever since, but I still remember that initial terror. I was surprised that "they" let me, a 22-year-old novice, take her home.

Who is this nebulous "they" we always want to defer to? Because the truth is, when it comes to children, no one is positioned better to love and do what's best for a child than her parents. No one loves her so much or has so much at stake. In fact, everyone else has their own interests at stake.

## This is a noble work

This is a noble work. When you take the reins of your children's educations, you don't just give your own child a better life. You affect every generation that comes after your children. Additionally, the influence of your child's education radiates outward, not just down through the family.

Every time a person thinks through an issue and ignores the mainstream media, an anchor has been set down. Instead of just floating downstream like everyone else, the critically thinking person makes everyone stop and take notice.

When Merianne Jensen's kids showed up at school without masks, other children started to ask why. When Traci Woodard's children followed their interests to the school that made sense, they became successful and confident. When the young men at Boys' Latin learned an ancient language at their inner-city school, their perspective broadened, and the people around them saw them in a different light.

When you save a child, you save a family—a future family. You may never have to throw yourself over your children as a tornado pummels your neighborhood, but you absolutely will need to protect them, prepare them, and teach them to thrive in their own culture. And the traditions you start might last for generations.

This is true not just with your own children but with other children, too.

When my dad was a little boy, an older neighbor used to say to him, "Wendell, I have a book I'd really like your opinion on. Would you mind reading it and then we could talk about it?"

She'd let him borrow the book and he'd return in a few days, ready to discuss the ideas in the book. She helped him cultivate a lifelong love of reading. To this day, my dad reads the best books, and he has certainly influenced my interests and learning, which have trickled down to my children.

Your influence is just as important as the neighbor lady who took an interest in a small boy named Wendell. Your commitment to education and culture can have lasting influence on your own children and everyone around you.

## How much does your reputation matter?

But here's a problem. You've worked hard to get along with people. You're agreeable, kind, generous to a fault. People like you, and if you stand up for your children or follow an unconventional route for their educations, you'll ruffle some feathers.

Merianne Jensen put it this way: "My reputation is not as important as my kids. And at this point, I will do anything for them. They can't fight this battle on their own, and, unfortunately, they're on the front line of the battle, and it's not their battle to fight. And it breaks my heart, and I will step in with swords and daggers and anything I can to help them."

Chances are not good that you'll need swords and daggers, but you might need tough skin. When I received that certified letter from a local law firm, I had never even had a speeding ticket before. I couldn't believe I was "in trouble."

Why do some people feel so threatened when parents reject the status quo and choose unconventional education options for their children?

There's a lot at stake for the education monopoly. Right now, they have a sweet deal. They get roughly $15,000 per child per year without ever having to prove that the child makes any academic progress. If a student fails to meet basic proficiency requirements, they can blame the parents or say they didn't have enough funding—they do this all the time.

When you pull a child out of the system, they lose $15,000 (much more in some places). They also lose credibility. Since the school shutdowns of 2020, millions of parents have found alternatives to district public schools. And this doesn't just affect funding for the schools. Because most teachers succumb to pressure to join teachers unions, enrollment also affects political donations. More than 99% of campaign contributions from teachers' unions go to Democrat candidates.

In short, parents face tremendous pressure to keep their children enrolled in the government schools. Each child counts toward keeping the monopoly machinery intact. Sadly, your child's education is linked to political campaigns and salaries for the ever-growing bureaucracies filled with administrators and staff.

But as a parent, your job is to put your child's interests ahead of everyone else's. Clearly, you're the only one who can (and will).

Just a few years ago, the notion of politicians instructing us to stay home, or the federal government printing trillions of dollars, thereby imposing inflation and high interest rates on citizens without their input, would have seemed unthinkable. The ideals we've refined through the ages have been challenged in unprecedented ways.

Giving your children a better education than you received is no small undertaking. Protecting them from the complexities of our current age may appear to be a daunting task. Rest assured, not only are you equal to this task, but you are also the sole person capable of making these essential decisions for your children.

It's completely natural to question ourselves as we navigate parenthood. However, let this serve as your reassurance: your dedication and love for your children's education are unparalleled, and nobody holds your children's well-being closer to heart than you do.

Every parent embarks on this journey with the purest intentions and aspirations for their children's future. Recognize that education is not a simple, linear path with guaranteed outcomes. Navigating K-12 education in today's America calls for adaptability, resilience, and courage. The choices you have made thus far were grounded in the information and resources at your disposal at the time. Though hindsight may reveal other options, it's important to remember that your decisions were made with your children's best interests in mind.

Don't fixate on the past. Learn from the past and steer your kids toward a more promising future. Even if your children are preparing to graduate, it's not too late to engage with their teachers and schools or to try your hand at a different educational mode altogether. Get involved in your children's education. In your home, cultivate a passion for learning and inspire your children to explore new areas of interest. Honor their unique selves and celebrate their distinct strengths. And, importantly, bear in mind that education is not a race; it is a lifelong, enriching journey.

## The 3 P's revisited

In shepherding a K-12 education, you are undertaking a monumental and often overwhelming task—one that carries immense responsibility and significance. The three P's (Protection, Preparation, and Paideia) can keep you focused on what matters most.

Firstly, Protection is paramount. In a rapidly changing world, your role as a guardian—shielding your children's physical, emotional, and intellectual well-being—is more vital than ever. This isn't about creating a bubble that isolates them from the world, but rather about cultivating a safe and nurturing environment in which they can grow and thrive, resilient and prepared for the challenges life will inevitably throw their way.

Preparation is your proactive approach to your child's future. It involves equipping your children with the tools, knowledge, and skills they need to navigate the world confidently and competently. It means not just preparing them for tests, but for life. It's about fostering independence, critical thinking, and a love for lifelong learning.

And then comes Paideia, the process of educating a child into becoming a thoughtful, informed, and active citizen. This is not education for the mere sake of knowledge, but education as the cultivation of a whole person. It is about fostering a sense of curiosity, ethics, and a deep appreciation for the world's array of knowledge and culture. It's the cultivation of a lifelong learner, a compassionate neighbor, a responsible citizen. Western civilization will survive to the extent that we teach our children to treasure it.

Remember, education is not just a phase; it's a foundational part of your child's life journey, and these three P's are the sturdy pillars upon which this journey is built. They are your compass, directing each step through the often-complex landscape of K-12 education.

The road ahead is long, and it won't always be smooth. But take heart in knowing that your earnest efforts in protection, preparation, and paideia are the most profound investments you could make in your child's future.

So, as you stand in the role of an educator, a guide, and most importantly, a parent—take a deep breath and stand tall. You are crafting not just an education, but a life rich with purpose, integrity, and wisdom.

You've got this.

This is a mighty task — perhaps the most significant work in the world. And what a privilege it is to be part of it. What, after all, matters more?

* * *

# Appendix

## *Handwriting Helps for Parents Kathleen S. Wright, Founder and Executive Director of The Handwriting Collaborative*

### Classroom and/or Home Activities to Improve Fine Motor Skill Development

PreK and early primary children benefit from experiences that support the development of fine motor skills in the hands and fingers. Children should have strength and dexterity in their hands and fingers before being asked to manipulate a pencil on paper. Working on dexterity and strength first can eliminate the development of an inappropriate pencil grasp, which is becoming more commonplace as young children are engaged in writing experiences before their hands are ready.

#### *Fine Motor Activities*

The following activities invclve the use of manipulatives which will support young children's fine motor development, and will help to build the strength and dexterity necessary to hold a pencil appropriately.

- Mold and roll play dough into balls - using the palms of the hands facing each other and with fingers curled slightly towards the palm.
- Roll play dough into tiny balls (peas) using only the fingertips.
- Use pegs or toothpicks to make designs in play dough.
- Cut play dough with a plastic knife or with a pizza or tracing wheel by holding the implement in a diagonal grasp.
- Tear newspaper into strips and then crumple them into balls. Use the balls of paper as stuffing for scare-crows, puppets, or other art projects.
- Scrunch up one (1) sheet of newspaper in one hand – great for building strength!
- Use a plant sprayer to spray plants, (indoors, out-doors) to spray snow (mix food coloring with water so that the snow can be painted), or melt "monsters". (Draw monster pictures with markers and the colors will run when sprayed.)
- Pick up objects using large tweezers such as those found in the "Bedbugs" game. This can be adapted by picking up Cheerios, small cubes, small marshmal-lows, pennies, etc., in counting games.
- Shake dice by cupping the hands together, forming an empty air space between the palms.
- Use small-sized screwdrivers like those found in an erector set.
- Use lacing and sewing activities such as stringing beads, Cheerios, macaroni, etc. (Also, if available, plastic-coated string works great with cut up drinking straws.)

- Use eye droppers to "pick up" colored water for color mixing or to make artistic designs on paper. Turn coffee filters into an art project!
- Roll small balls out of tissue paper, and then glue the balls onto construction paper to form pictures or designs.
- Attempt to turn over cards, coins, checkers, or buttons, without bringing them to the edge of the table.
- Make pictures using stickers or self-sticking paper (O) reinforcements.
- Play games with the "puppet fingers" -thumb, index, and middle fingers. At circle time have each child's puppet fingers tell about what happened over the weekend, or use them in songs and finger plays.

### *Scissor Activities*

When scissors are held correctly, and when they fit a child's hand well, cutting activities will exercise the very same muscles which are needed to manipulate a pencil in a mature tripod grasp. The correct scissor position is with the thumb and middle finger in the handles of the scissors, the index finger on the outside of the handle to stabilize, with fingers four and five curled into the palm.

- Cut up junk mail or magazine subscription cards.
- Make fringe on the edge of a piece of construction paper.
- Cut play dough with scissors.
- Cut straws or shredded paper.

## Sensory Activities

The following activities ought to be done frequently to increase large muscle strength and endurance. These activities also strengthen the child's awareness of his/her hands.

- Wheelbarrow walking, crab walking
- Clapping games (loud/quiet, on knees, together, etc.)
- Catching (clapping) bubbles between hands
- Draw in a tactile medium such as wet sand, salt, rice, or "goop". Make "goop" by adding colored water to cornstarch until you have a mixture similar in consistency to toothpaste. The "drag" of this mixture provides feedback to the muscle and joint receptors, thus facilitating visual motor control.
- Pick out small objects like pegs, beads, coins, etc., from a tray of salt, sand, rice, or putty. Try it with eyes closed too. This helps develop sensory awareness in the hands.

## Midline Crossing

The establishment of hand dominance may still be developing. Until it does, a child may switch hands at the midline when doing certain activities. The following activities are intended to help facilitate midline crossing:

Encourage reaching across the body for materials with each hand. It may be necessary to engage the other hand in an activity to prevent switching hands at midline.

Refrain specifically from discouraging a child from using the left hand for any activity. Allow for the natural development of hand dominance by presenting activities at midline and allowing the child to choose freely.

- Start making the child aware of the left and right sides of his body through spontaneous comments like, "kick the ball with your right leg."
- Play imitation posture games like "Simon Says" with across the body movements.
- When painting at an easel, encourage the child to paint a continuous line across the entire paper. Then also one from diagonal to diagonal.

## Activities for the Development of Handwriting Skills

There are significant prerequisites for writing skills which begin in infancy and continue to emerge through the preschool years. The following activities support and promote fine motor and visual motor development:

### *Body Stability*

The joints of the body need to be stable before the hands can be free to focus on specific skilled fine motor tasks. Activities include:

- Wheelbarrow walking, crab walking, and wall push-ups.
- Using toys like Silly Putty ; and outside play with equipment like monkey bars on the playground.
- Throwing a ball through an old tire or at a cardboard target.
- Dancing or marching to music.

## *Fine Motor Skills*

- When a certain amount of body stability has developed, the hands and fingers begin to work on movements of dexterity and isolation as well as different kinds of grasps. Children will develop fine motor skills best when they work on a VERTICAL or near vertical surface as much as possible. (i.e. chalkboard, whiteboard, 3" desk binder) In particular, the wrist must be bent back in the direction of the hand.
- Attach a large piece of drawing paper to the wall. Have the child use a large marker and try the following exercises to develop visual motor skills: Make a letter, number, or letter part (stroke) model - one per sheet of paper. Have the child trace over your line from left to right, or from top to bottom. Have them trace over each figure at least 10 times. Then have the child draw their figure next to your model several times.
- Play connect the dots. Again make sure the child's strokes connect the dots from left to right, and from top to bottom.
- Trace around stencils - the non-dominant hand should hold the stencil flat and stable against the paper, while the dominant hand pushes the pencil firmly against the edge of the stencil. *The stencil must be held firmly.*
- Attach a large piece of felt to the wall, or use a felt board. The child can use felt shapes to make pictures. Magnetic boards can be used the same way.
- Have the child work on a chalkboard doing the same kinds of tracing and modeling activities as suggested above.
- Paint at an easel. Some of the modeling activities as suggested above can be done at the easel.

### *Ocular Motor Control*

This refers to the ability of the eyes to work together to follow and hold an object in the line of vision as needed.

- Use a flashlight against the ceiling. Have the child lie on his/her back or tummy and visually follow the moving light from left to right, top to bottom, and diagonally.
- Find hidden pictures in books, or magazines like "Highlights for Children."
- Practice maze activities.

### *Eye-hand Coordination*

This involves accuracy in placement, direction, and spatial awareness.

- Throw bean bags/koosh balls into a hula hoop placed flat on the floor. Gradually increase the distance.
- Play throw and catch with a ball . Start with a large ball and work toward a smaller ball. (Koosh balls are easier to catch than a tennis ball.)
- Practice hitting bowling pins with a ball. (You can purchase these games or make your own with soda bottles and a small ball.)
- Play "Hit the Balloon" with a medium-sized balloon.

## Recommended Books and Articles

Berk, L.E. (1989). *Child Development*. Boston, Mass.: Allyn and Bacon.

Clare, L., and H. Garnier. (2000). Parents' goals for adolescents diagnosed with developmental delays in early childhood. *Journal of Early Adolescence*, 20(4), 442-446.

Hammet, C.T. (1992). *Movement Activities for Early Childhood.* Champaign, Ill.: Human Kinetics.

Kristensen, N. (2001). *Basic Parenting Focus Issue: Motor Development.* Minneapolis, Minn.: Family Information Services.

Malina, R.M., and C. Bouchard. (1991). *Growth, Maturation, and Physical Activity*. Champaign, Ill.: Human Kinetics.

http://www.education.com/reference/article/Ref_Supporting_Physical/

Mayesky, M. (1999). *Creative Activities for Children*. Thomson Publishing.

# End Notes

1. Harper Keenan & Lil Miss Hot Mess (2020) Drag pedagogy: The playful practice of queer imagination in early childhood, Curriculum Inquiry, 50:5, 440-461, DOI: 10.1080/03626784.2020.1864621

2. Olza, Ibone et al. "Women's psychological experiences of physiological childbirth: a meta-synthesis." *BMJ open* vol. 8,10 e020347. 18 Oct. 2018, doi:10.1136/bmjopen-2017-020347

3. White, Tracie. "Epidurals Increase in Popularity, Stanford Study Finds." *Scope*, 26 June 2018.

4. *Highest C-Section Rates By Country | BellyBelly*. 30 Nov. 2016, https://www.bellybelly.com.au/birth/highest-c-section-rates-by-country/.

5. Mendelsohn, Robert S. Male Practice: How Doctors Manipulate Women. Chicago: Contemporary Books, Inc., 1981. p. 151

6. *Middle District of Florida | Doctor, Pharmacists, And Marketers In Compounding Pharmacy Kickback Conspiracy Sentenced | United States Department of Justice*. 19 Dec. 2019, https://www.justice.gov/usao-mdfl/pr/doctor-pharmacists-and-marketers-compounding-pharmacy-kickback-conspiracy-sentenced.

7. *District of New Jersey | Pharmaceutical Company Agrees to Pay $3.5 Million to Resolve Allegations of Violating False Claims Act | United States Department of Justice*. 28 July 2020, https://www.justice.gov/usao-nj/pr/pharmaceutical-company-agrees-pay-35-million-resolve-allegations-violating-false-claims.

8. Hoekelman, R. A. "Well-Child Visits Revisited." *American Journal of Diseases of Children (1960)* 137, no. 1 (January 1983): 17–20. https://doi.org/10.1001/archpedi.1983.02140270013005.

9. Simmering, Jacob E., Linnea A. Polgreen, Joseph E. Cavanaugh, and Philip M. Polgreen. "Are Well-Child Visits a Risk Factor for Subsequent Influenza-like Illness Visits?" *Infection Control and Hospital Epidemiology* 35, no. 3 (March 2014): 251–56. https://doi.org/10.1086/675281.

10. *HonorHealth - Frequently Asked Questions*. https://www.honorhealth.com/contact-us/frequently-asked-questions#mychartfaq. Accessed 17 Aug. 2023.

11. "Amanda Wray on X." *Twitter*, 23 June 2022, https://twitter.com/AmandaWray/status/1539775961578606593.

12. https://strongnebraska.org/blog/member/sherwood-foundation/#:~:text=The%20Sherwood%20Foundation%20promotes%20equity,quality%20of%20life%20in%20Nebraska.

13. Ingraham, Christopher. "There's Never Been a Safer Time to Be a Kid in America." *Washington Post*, November 25, 2021. https://www.washingtonpost.com/news/wonk/wp/2015/04/14/theres-never-been-a-safer-time-to-be-a-kid-in-america/.

14. https://www.npr.org/2022/09/12/1121999705/sex-education-school-kindergarten

15. Magazine, Smithsonian, and Colin Schultz. "No, You're Probably Not Smarter Than a 1912-Era 8th Grader." Smithsonian Magazine. Accessed May 11, 2023. https://www.smithsonianmag.com/smart-news/no-youre-probably-not-smarter-than-a-1912-era-8th-grader-19949041/.

16. "How COVID-19 School Closures Sparked a Parent Movement Driving Politics Three Years On." Restoring America, March 13, 2023. https://www.washingtonexaminer.com/restoring-america/community-family/how-covid-19-school-closures-sparked-a-parent-movement-driving-politics-three-years-on.

17. Remnick, David. "Jonathan Haidt Wants You to Take Away Your Kid's Phone." *The New Yorker*, 20 Apr. 2024. *www.newyorker.com*, https://www.newyorker.com/news/the-new-yorker-interview/jonathan-haidt-wants-you-to-take-away-your-kids-phone.

18. https://smartphonefreechildhood.co.uk/

19. Reynolds, Glenn Harlan. "Stolen Youth: An Interview with Karol Markowicz and Bethany Mandel." *Glenn's*

*Substack*, 8 Mar. 2023, https://instapundit.substack.com/p/stolen-youth-an-interview-with-karol.

20. "Courts to Determine If Schools Can Hide Information From Parents About Their Kids - Intellectual Takeout," June 20, 2022. https://intellectualtakeout.org/2022/06/courts-to-determine-if-schools-can-hide-information-from-parents-about-their-kids/.

21. Alonso, Melissa. "Florida Teacher Says She Is under Investigation after Showing 5th Grade Class Disney Movie with Gay Character." CNN, May 15, 2023. https://www.cnn.com/2023/05/15/us/florida-teacher-disney-movie-gay/index.html.

22. Libs of TikTok [@libsoftiktok]. "Florida Teacher in @HernandoSchools Says Parents Don't Have Rights in Their Children's Education: 'Rights as a Parent, Those Rights Are Gone When Your Child Is in the Public School System.' Https://T.Co/WcZRhReuHY." Tweet. *Twitter*, May 16, 2023. https://twitter.com/libsoftiktok/status/1658552802249940994.

23. Delaney, Matt. "Tennessee Soccer Coach Arrested on Child Abuse Charges." *Washington Times*, 10 July 2023, https://html5-player.libsyn.com/embed/episode/id/27780075/height/90/theme/custom/thumbnail/yes/direction/backward/no-cache/true/render-playlist/yes/custom-color/b5101f/destination_id/1419779.

24. "Transgender Marxism." *Pluto Press*, https://www.plutobooks.com/9780745341668/transgender-marxism. Accessed 17 Aug. 2023.

25. *Forum Guide to Protecting the Privacy of Student Information: State and Local Education Agencies - 6.B. Release of Directory Information*. National Center for Education Statistics, https://nces.ed.gov/pubs2004/privacy/section_6b.asp. Accessed 25 Oct. 2024.

26. "U.S. Students' Academic Achievement Still Lags That of Their Peers in Many Other Countries." *Pew Research Center*, https://www.pewresearch.org/short-reads/2017/02/15/u-s-students-internationally-math-science/. Accessed 17 Aug. 2023.

27. *Social Emotional Learning Was Always a Bad Idea | Frontpage Mag*. 10 May 2022, https://www.frontpagemag.com/social-emotional-learning-was-always-bad-idea-larry-sand/.

28. Velásquez, Lizzie. "Lizzie Velásquez: How Do You Define Yourself? | TED Talk." Accessed May 22, 2023. https://www.ted.com/talks/lizzie_velasquez_how_do_you_define_yourself.

29. "UPDATE: Lincoln Teacher Arrested for Sexual Assault of 14-Year-o." *KLKN-TV*, 19 Mar. 2015, https://www.klkntv.com/lincoln-teacher-arrested-for-sexual-assault/.

30. *Former Irving Teacher Gets 20-30 Years in Sex Assault of Student*. https://journalstar.com/news/local/crime-and-courts/former-irving-teacher-gets-20-30-years-in-sex-assault-of-student/

article_4d092136-75cf-57e4-b29a-dfff5047360d.html#tncms-source=login. Accessed 17 Aug. 2023.

31. Reist, Margaret. "Duncan Responds to Terry's Call for Investigation at Irving." *JournalStar.Com*, 25 Mar. 2015, https://journalstar.com/news/local/education/duncan-responds-to-terrys-call-for-investigation-at-irving/article_510c57b8-6747-55da-933a-cb1a3785fc35.html.

32. *Sexual Abuse of Students in Schools Is Something Every Parents Should Worry about | Fox News.* https://www.foxnews.com/opinion/sexual-abuse-students-schools-parent-worry-christopher-rufo. Accessed 17 Aug. 2023.

33. "Too Pretty for Prison: No Jail Time for Tampa Teacher Debra LaFave." *Wtsp.Com*, 22 Nov. 2005, https://www.wtsp.com/article/news/local/too-pretty-for-prison-no-jail-time-for-tampa-teacher-debra-lafave/67-396101001.

34. Jones, Mydrim. "Teen Took Own Life after Being Molested by Sex-Crazed Female Teacher." *Mirror*, 16 Mar. 2019, https://www.mirror.co.uk/news/us-news/humiliated-teen-took-life-after-14145582.

35. "Crime Stories with Nancy Grace: Molestation, Bullying at School. Protect Your Child, 'Don't Be A Victim' on Apple Podcasts." *Apple Podcasts*, https://podcasts.apple.com/us/podcast/molestation-bullying-at-school-protect-your-child-dont/

id1193068130?i=1000492845751. Accessed 17 Aug. 2023.

36. Hannon, Elliot. "New Test Scores Show U.S. Students Continue to Trail Global Peers in Reading and Math." *Slate*, 3 Dec. 2019. *slate.com*, https://slate.com/news-and-politics/2019/12/global-test-scores-us-american-students-performance-trail-reading-math-science.html.

37. "Dumbing Down K-12 Education." *American Center for Transforming Education*, 10 Sept. 2021, https://www.discovery.org/education/2021/09/10/dumbing-down-k-12-education/.

38. https://www.analyze-ed.com/average-act-score.html

39. Chuminski, Jedrzej. "Formy Nadzoru Srodowiska Pracowników Przemyslu W Latach Forsownej Industrializacji (1949-1956): The Forms of Control of Industrial Workers in the Years of Intensive Industrialization, 1949-56." *Studia Historyczne* 41, no. 4 (October 1998): 557–75.

40. Pullmann, Joy, and Dr Sumantra Maitra. *'Witches' and 'Viruses:' The Activist-Academic Threat and a Policy Response*. 3630654, 18 June 2020. *Social Science Research Network*, https://doi.org/10.2139/ssrn.3630654.

41. Parsons, Nicholas T. THE LONG MARCH THROUGH THE INSTITUTIONS – DOUGLAS MURRAY'S BOOK ON OUR CIVILIZATION AND ITS DISCONTENTS | Hungarian Review. 7 May 2020, https://hungarianreview.com/article/

20200515 the long march through the institutions douglas murray s book on our civilization and its discontents/.

42. "The Left's Long March Through The Institutions Is Now Pretty Much Complete, And It's A Disaster." *Center for Individualism*, 19 May 2019, https://centerforindividualism.org/the-lefts-long-march-through-the-institutions-is-now-pretty-much-complete-and-its-a-disaster/.

43. "The Well-Trained Mind, 4th Edition." *Well-Trained Mind*, 14 July 2021, https://welltrainedmind.com/p/well-trained-mind-4th-edition/.

44. *Classical Education with Jeremy Tate.* https://www.2centdad.com/classical-education-with-jeremy-tate/. Accessed 17 Aug. 2023.

45. Alias. "The Benefits of a Classical Education." *The New American*, 26 July 2013, https://thenewamerican.com/us/education/the-benefits-of-a-classical-education/.

46. Richard M Weaver. *Richard M. Weaver Ideas Have Consequences University Of Chicago Press*. 1999. *Internet Archive*, http://archive.org/details/richard-m.-weaver-ideas-have-consequences-university-of-chicago-press.

47. Wisdom and Eloquence: A Christian Paradigm for Classical Learning. Robert Littlejohn & Charles T. Evans, Crossway Books, 2006. p. 29 (Call Number LC 368.L58 2006) ↑

48. Classical Education in Britain 1500-1900 by M. L. Clarke, Cambridge at the University Press, 1959, 1.

49. Bolgar, R. R. "Classical Education in Britain, 1500–1900. By M. L. Clarke. Cambridge University Press, 1959. Pp. 234. 32s. 6d." *The Historical Journal*, vol. 2, no. 2, June 1959, pp. 189–91. *Cambridge University Press*, https://doi.org/10.1017/S0018246X0002210X.

50. "The Growing Movement to Restore Classical Education." *Washington Examiner*, 24 June 2022, https://www.washingtonexaminer.com/opinion/the-growing-movement-to-restore-classical-education.

51. "The Growing Movement to Restore Classical Education." *Washington Examiner*, 24 June 2022, https://www.washingtonexaminer.com/opinion/the-growing-movement-to-restore-classical-education.

52. De Pourcq, Maarten. "'The Paideia of the Greeks': On the Methodology of Roland Barthes's Comment Vivre Ensemble." *Paragraph* 31, no. 1 (March 2008): 23–37. https://doi.org/10.3366/E0264833408000047.

53. Hicks, David. Norms & Nobility: A Treatise on Education. Praeger, 1981, 22.

54. Origio, Iris. "The Education of Renaissance Man." Horizon 2 (January 1960): 57-73.

55. Liu, Justin Perkins |. photo by James. "After Graduate Is Charged with Sexual Assault, Education College Reaffirms Dedication to Integrity." *The Daily Nebraskan*, 31 Mar. 2015, https://www.dailyne-

braskan.com/news/after-graduate-is-charged-with-sexual-assault-education-college-reaffirms-dedication-to-integrity/article_a17d7ea8-d74c-11e4-be14-437623e64f34.html.

56. *Classical Education with Jeremy Tate.* https://www.2centdad.com/classical-education-with-jeremy-tate/. Accessed 17 Aug. 2023.

57. *Cursive Comeback Why It's Not Taught in All CO Schools and Why Teaching It May Be Vital.* Directed by KRDO NewsChannel 13, 2021. *YouTube*, https://www.youtube.com/watch?v=c_T18zo3f2k.

58. Supon, Vi. 2009. "Cursive Writing: Are Its Last Days Approaching?" *Journal of Instructional Psychology* 36 (4): 357–59. https://search-ebscohost-com.byu.idm.oclc.org/login.aspx?direct=true&db=eric&AN=EJ952289&site=ehost-live&scope=site.

59. Rufo, D. (2004). Is teaching cursive writing a waste of time? It's a 'loopy' use of class time. American Teacher, 88(6), 4. Retrieved February 12, 2009, from Education Full Text database.

60. "The Letters of Italo Calvino." *The New Yorker*, 8 May 2013. *www.newyorker.com*, https://www.newyorker.com/books/page-turner/the-letters-of-italo-calvino.

# About the Author

Rachel Terry teaches writing at Brigham Young University, where she is completing her Master's degree in English. She has written ten books, including study guides and educational materials, along with articles for various publications.

Connect on X: @_rachelterry_

www.ingramcontent.com/pod-product-compliance
Lightning Source LLC
Chambersburg PA
CBHW061739120626
46550CB00005B/1830

*9781965113042*